Alone With God

Dom Jean Leclercq

A L O N E

W I T H

G O D

New York

FARRAR, STRAUS AND CUDAHY

Translated by Elizabeth McCabe
from the French, *Seul avec
Dieu: La Vie Erémitique*

IMPRIMI POTEST: Dom Jacques Winandy
Abbot of Claravalle
September 8, 1955

IMPRIMATUR: Michael Potevin
Vicar General
Paris, September 14, 1955

Library of Congress Catalog Card Number: 61-11318

CONTENTS

distinguished from every kind of secular (even if solitary) life. By his vows, the hermit belongs to a state of life approved by the Church, and his whole life is worship of God. The hermit's religious life is contemplative, rather than active; the relative value of these two vocations is apparent from their distinctive functions. Eremitical life in the history of Christianity; how it differs from cenobitic life; how closely the two ways are connected.

False vocations: an illusion which must be discouraged. A true vocation is a call from Christ, who alone must be followed; not men, even if they be saints. The signs of Christ's call. A vocation implies the obligation of following it despite all obstacles, and it confers strength as needed.

A frequent objection is that the hermit life is useless. The answer lies in the law of each man's fidelity to his own vocation. The hermit "proclaims God's kingdom" by renouncing the world for the sake of the kingdom of Heaven. The meaning of religious profession in this context. Through the communion of saints, the hermit's personal sanctification helps his neighbor. The contemplative life produces a rich harvest. Why Blessed Giustiniani seldom refers to the prayer of intercession.

Part Two: THE HERMIT LIFE

Part Three: THE HERMIT'S PRAYER

Part Four: THE HERMIT'S ASCETICISM

Part Five: UNIVERSAL LOVE AS
THE ULTIMATE GOAL

Blessed Giustiniani's mystical doctrine is
based on his personal experience. Profound
humility is the condition for union with
God. Prayers for the grace of self-knowledge. Trust in God springs from the realization of our own worthlessness. God raises
up those who fall through Christ, who is
the way of our return to God. The need to
attain the absolute humility of Jesus, who
sought only His Father's glory. The four
kinds of self-effacement. We may truly lose
ourselves in God through the Eucharist.

A soul united to God by love becomes
transformed in Him without being identi-
fied with Him and without alienating its
own nature. Explanations and comparisons
which elucidate this mystery. The practical
consequences of such perfect love: total renouncement of self, the seeking of God's
glory for its own sake alone, the acceptance
of all suffering that glorifies God. The orthodoxy of this mystical teaching which is,
however, inadequate to translate an experience that is ineffable.

Love of God is the only fulfillment of the
command to love our neighbor. We love
ourselves and our neighbor perfectly when
our love is in no slightest degree deflected
from God. Comparisons explaining this:
God is One and the same Being in Himself
and in His creatures; God loves Himself
and His creatures with the same love. The
union of creatures with God. Christ, model
of universal love. Sonnet on "The Presence
of God."

Like martyrdom, the eremitical vocation
bears witness to Jesus Christ. Hermit life is
a martyrdom because it implies total renouncement. He who loves God alone
dwells in changeless peace with God, with
himself, and with all creatures. But his
peace is "the peace of Christ," that is, the
cross of Christ joyfully accepted.

PREFACE

By THOMAS MERTON

Just as the Church of God can never be without
martyrs, so too she can never be without solitaries,
for the hermit, like the martyr, is the most eloquent
witness of the Risen Christ. It was on the night of
Easter that the Risen Savior breathed upon His
Apostles, that they might receive of His Spirit,
Who had not been given before because Christ was
not yet glorified. St. Paul has told us that all who
are sons of God are activated and moved by the
Spirit of God. They have the Spirit of Christ because they belong to Christ. Having His Spirit, they
live no longer according to the flesh but according
to the Spirit. *Qui vero secundum Spiritum sunt,
quae sunt Spiritus sentiunt.*[1] Therefore they are of
one mind and one Spirit with Jesus Christ.

---

[1] Rom. 8:5 ["To live the life of the spirit is to think the
thoughts of the spirit."]

Now at the beginning of His public life, Jesus was led into the desert by the Spirit, that He might engage in single combat with the devil. The struggle in the desert was the prelude to the struggle in the Garden of the Agony. This last was the exemplar and meritorious cause of the charity of all the martyrs and all the hermits who would be tested, like Christ himself, in the furnace of tribulation because they were pleasing to God. The Church of God, triumphing in her martyrs and ascetics, would thus be able to declare with Christ Himself: "The prince of this world indeed comes, and he has no part in me: but he comes that the world may know that I love the Father!"[2]

There must, therefore, be hermits. Nor is this only because there will always be men who desire solitude. The Christian hermit is one who is led into the desert by the Spirit, not by the flesh, even though he may well have a natural inclination to live alone. Our own time has seen hermits like the Dominican, Père Vayssière, who entered the Order of Preachers knowing that he wanted to preach the Gospel, and completely unaware that he would spend most of his life in solitude at La Sainte Baume. Nor must there always be hermits, merely because there are always contemplative souls, or because the contemplative naturally seeks physical solitude: (for without the efficacious desire of exterior soli-

---

[2] John 14:30-31.

tude, interior solitude will always remain a fantasy or an illusion.) The true reason for the persistence of hermits even in ages which are most hostile to the solitary ideal is that the exigencies of Christian life *demand* that there be hermits. The Kingdom of God would be incomplete without them, for they are the men who seek God alone with the most absolute and undaunted and uncompromising singleness of heart. If we have forgotten that the Fathers of the Church assigned to the hermit a high, even the highest place among all Christian vocations, a modern theologian, Dom Anselm Stolz, is there to remind us of the fact.[3] And now another Benedictine, Dom Jean Leclercq, has added an important volume to the slowly growing collection of works on the solitary life appearing in our own time.

This book is all the more important because it introduces us to a hermit as interesting as he is unknown: a surprising figure, rising up almost unaccountably in the Italy of Raphael and Machiavelli, Castiglione and Michelangelo Buonarotti. Paul Giustiniani, as we learn from the brief note on his life which opens the author's introduction, became a novice at Camaldoli in 1510—that is to say that he entered the most ancient of the eremitical Orders that have survived in the Western Church. Camaldoli goes back to the tenth century and Saint Ro-

[3] In *L'ascèse chrétienne* (Chevetogne, 1948).

muald. Less famous than the Chartreuse, Camaldoli nevertheless has retained more of the aspect of an ancient *"laura"* than we would find in any Chartreuse. The Camaldolese idea is simply to apply the Rule of St. Benedict to the eremitical life. St. Benedict declared, of course, that his Rule was written for cenobites, but he also holds the solitary life in high honor, and suggests that certain monks, after a long probation in the monastery, may be called by God to a hermitage. St. Romuald made it possible for monks to have solitude without losing anything of the *bonum obedientiae* which is the treasure of monastic life, and without departing from that life in common, the life of fraternal charity which is the security of all who do not feel themselves equal to the heroism of another Anthony. The *Sacro Eremo* of Camaldoli is, therefore, a community of hermits, a village of ancient cells hidden in a pine forest several thousand feet above sea level in the Appennines behind Arezzo.

Paul Giustiniani entered Camaldoli at a time when the fervor had lost some of its ancient heat, and he left it for a stricter solitude. Eventually he was to start a new eremitical Congregation of his own, the Hermits of Monte Corona, who stall have a community at Frascati outside Rome, and several others in Italy, Spain, Poland, and the United States.[4]

---

[4] A new foundation, which is located near McConnelsville, Ohio, was established in September, 1959.

Giustiniani thus bears the same relation to Camaldoli as the Abbé de Rancé does to the Order of Citeaux, and, in another sense, as Dom Innocent Le Masson does to the Chartreuse. Like each of these great men, Paul Giustiniani seeks to rekindle the ancient fire that is burning low in an age that has no love for asceticism, for contemplation, or for solitude. It is therefore of the greatest interest to have at our disposal a volume that brings together from his various works, most of which are inaccessible, a complete doctrine of the solitary life.

Let us now turn to the doctrine of Blessed Paul, whose name recalls to our minds the half-legendary figure of the "first hermit" whom St. Anthony is supposed to have discovered in the cave where he had lived for over a hundred years unknown to men. The eremitical life is above all solitary. St. Romuald chose to settle in the once inviolable forest of Camaldoli and to seek God in a solitude that was *sacred*, that is to say entirely consecrated to Him. The inviolable character of "holy solitude" is a witness to the infinite transcendence of Him whose holiness elevates Him above all things. In order to seek Him Who is inaccessible the hermit himself becomes inaccessible. But within the little village of cells centered about the Church of the *Eremo* is a yet more perfect solitude: that of each hermit's own cell. Within the cell is the hermit himself, in the solitude of his own soul. But—and this is the ultimate test of solitude—the hermit is not alone

with himself: for that would not be a sacred lone-
liness. Holiness is life. Holy solitude is nourished
with the Bread of Life and drinks deep at the very
Fountain of all Life. The solitude of a soul enclosed within itself is death. And so the authentic,
the really sacred solitude is the infinite solitude of
God Himself, Alone, in Whom the hermits are
alone.

From this obligation to seek interior solitude flow
all the other demands made upon the hermit, the
other essential obligations of his state: silence, stability, recollection, mortification, labor, fasting,
vigils and prayer. These detach the soul from all
that is not God. They are not peculiar to the hermit. They belong to the monastic life wherever it
is found. But the hermit has a very special obligation to practise them, without, however, departing
from discretion which is one of the most important
virtues of the solitary. After all, it is discretion
which teaches us to live by the interior guidance of
the Holy Spirit. It is discretion which teaches us to
distinguish between the voice of the Spirit and the
voice of the flesh or of the evil one. Discretion does
not permit us to be cowards, but neither does it
allow us to fall headlong into the abyss of vanity,
pride, or presumption. Without discretion, the solitary life ends fatally in disaster. In the true spirit of
St. Benedict, Paul Giustiniani declares that even
in the hermitage the best mortifications are those
which are not of our own choice, and that even the

hermit should seek to please God more by great fidelity in his ordinary duties than by extraordinary feats of ascetic heroism. The life of the solitary will be a continual warfare, in which the flesh fights not only against the spirit but against the flesh itself and in which the spirit also fights not only against flesh but even against the spirit. It is here, in this inexpressible rending of his own poverty, that the hermit enters, like Christ, into the area where he wages the combat that can never be told to anyone. This is the battle that is seen by no one except God, and whose vicissitudes are so terrible that when victory comes at last, the total poverty and emptiness of the victor are so absolute that there is no longer any place in his heart for pride.

Such is the *eremitica puritas* which opens the way for contemplation. Without this "annihilation" the solitary might perhaps be tempted to seek rest in the consolations of God for their own sake. He might enjoy a selfish and self-complacent solitude in which he was delivered from responsibilities and inundated with supernatural favors. In words that remind us of St. John of the Cross, Paul Giustiniani speaks of the false contemplatives who "are displeased by everything that deprives them of the rest they think they have found in God but which they seek, really, in themselves. Their only care is to seek after peace, not in things below them, not in themselves, but in God; however they desire this peace not for the glory of God, but out of love for themselves."[5]

Nor does the sacredness of solitude and the true eremitical purity allow the hermit to become absorbed in a zeal that does not extend beyond the welfare or reputation of his own monastery and his own Order, still less beyond his own progress and his own virtues. A life alone with God is something too vast to include such limited objectives within its range. It reaches up to God Himself, and in doing so, embraces the whole Church of God. Meanwhile, the hermit supports this interior poverty of spirit with the greatest exterior poverty. He must live like the poorest of the poor. *Eremitica puritas* is the peace of one who is content with bare necessities. Such peace is impossible where poverty is a mere matter of exterior form. The hermit is not one who, though deprived of the right to possess them, actually has the use of better objects and enjoys more plentiful comforts than could ever be afforded by the materially poor. The eremitical community itself must be a poor community. And although this simplicity guarantees the hermit a high place in the Church, he himself will remember that his elevation is in reality a matter of humility and abjection. He takes no part in the active affairs of the Church because he is too poor to merit a place in them. For him to accept prelacy would be

---

[5] *Cf.*, p. 0151.

an infidelity because it would be an act of presumption. Paul Giustiniani pursues this subject of poverty into the most remote corners of the hermit's soul. The solitary will not even pride himself on his strict observances, or compare himself with religious of other Orders. He will avoid the supreme folly of those who, having nothing in the world but their humility, lose even that by boasting of it! By this perfect forgetfulness of himself, the hermit merits to be called the successor of the martyrs.

There is a positive side to all this. Solitude is not sought for its own sake. If the eremitical life is the highest form of Christianity it is because the hermit aspires more than anyone else to perfect union with Christ. Jesus Himself is the living Rule of the hermit, just as He is the model of every religious. It is Christ Himself who calls us into solitude, exacting of us a clean break with the world and with our past, just as He did of St. Anthony. Perhaps more than any other the solitary life demands the presence of the Man Christ Who lives and suffers in us. Even if we worshipped the one true God in the desert, without the Incarnate Word our solitude would be less than human and therefore far short of the divine: without Him no one comes to the Father. Without Jesus we all too easily fulfil the words of Pascal that *"qui veut faire l'ange, fait la bête."* Solitude therefore must translate itself into the three words: *cum Christo vivere*—to live with Christ. Solitude is a fortress that protects the heart against all that is not Christ, and its only function is to allow Christ to live in us. Solitude spiritualizes the whole man, transforms him, body and soul, from a carnal to a spiritual being. It can only do so in the Spirit of Christ Who elevates our whole being in God, and does not divide man's personality against itself like those false asceticisms which St. Paul knew to be enemies of the Cross of Christ.

In a hymn to this solitude which is "too unknown," Giustiniani says: "It is thou that announcest the coming of the Holy Spirit: and not only announcest Him, but bringest Him into the human heart just as the dawn, which announces the day, brings to our eyes the brightness of the sun."[6]

This brings us to the mystical doctrine of Paul Giustiniani who, like the Fathers of the Church, believed that the eremitical life was ordered exclusively for contemplation and was the only purely contemplative life. Like the Fathers, also, when he speaks of contemplation he means mystical contemplation. This is without doubt the most interesting and important part of the book. In pages that remind us now of St. Catherine of Genoa, now of St. Bernard, now even of John Ruysbroeck, Paul Giustiniani teaches us a doctrine elevated but sure, since his whole emphasis is on the coincidence of humility and greatness in the experience of union. The way of contemplation is never exalted, and the

---

[6] *Cf.*, p. 061.

hermit must aspire to be "lifted up" in no other way than on the Cross, with Christ. He does not reach the Father except through the abjection of Christ, Who lives again in the hermit, that *exinanivit seme-tipsum* by which He merited for us a share in His sonship and in His divine glory. Reading the pages of Giustiniani on annihilation, we are reminded of St. John of the Cross, who describes the soul that is purified and ready for union with God in these terms:

"In this detachment the spiritual soul finds its quiet and repose; for, since it covets nothing, nothing wearies it when it is lifted up, and nothing oppresses it when it is cast down, because it is in the centre of its humility; but when it covets anything, at that very moment it becomes wearied."[7]

The whole purpose of the solitary life is to bring the soul into "the center of her humility" and to keep it there. The hermit does not pretend to have acquired any esoteric secret or any exalted technique by which he penetrates into the mystery of God. His only secret is the humility and poverty of Christ and the knowledge that God lifts up those who have fallen: *Dominus erigit elisos*. Without this humility, the contemplative can be a prey to "all the illusions." For "the true servants of Christ love God with all their being, and do not love them-

---

[7] *The Ascent of Mount Carmel*, I, chap. 13, in *The Complete Works of St. John of the Cross*, translated by Allison Peers (Burns & Oates, 1935), I, p. 60.

selves at all. They keep themselves so perfectly under the guardianship of humility as to be known by God alone, but unknown to men."[8]

But once he is perfectly united with the poverty and humility of Christ crucified, the solitary lives entirely by the life and Spirit of Christ. He can therefore be transformed and elevated to the perfection of selfless love for God, that love in which he no longer knows himself or anything else, but only God alone. This is the culmination of mystical love in which the contemplative "loves God in God." It is here that we detect interesting resonances from the doctrine of Ruysbroeck. Whether or not Giustiniani knew the Flemish mystic, a comparison between them might be interesting. This is not the place for it. What is more important here is to notice that this love for God in God, which is the highest perfection of the solitary and contemplative life is also the perfect justification of the hermit's utility to the rest of the Church.

The hermit is not to be considered a "dynamo" of apostolic power in the crude sense of a machine actively producing a great quantity of prayers and works or penance for the salvation of souls. We have seen that quantity becomes a negligible factor in the life of *eremitica puritas*. The solitary should not seek to replace his lost possessions by merely numerical accumulation of prayers and good works

---

[8] *Cf.*, p. 0142.

over which he can gloat like a happy miser at the end. In praying to God for souls, he realizes it is not so important to know the souls for whom he is praying, as *Him to Whom* he is praying. But the perfect love of God teaches him to find souls in God Himself. He discovers that the soul which is on fire with love for God actually loves herself and other men more in proportion as she thinks about herself and them less. Hence the paradox that the less the contemplative seems to love others and himself, the more he forgets them in order to direct all his love to God, the more he actually loves them and the better he serves their spiritual interests. Loving God in God, the solitary is perfectly united to that infinite Love with which God loves all things in Himself. Loving all things in Him, the hermit powerfully cooperates with the action of His love, drawing them to Himself. Thus he fulfils most efficaciously the purpose of his divine vocation which is to restore all things in Christ. Consequently the fruitfulness of the hermit in the Church of God depends on his fidelity to the call to solitude, obscurity, and abjection in Christ.

The doctrine of Paul Giustiniani is, therefore, a striking testimony to the primacy of contemplation and of the contemplative life in the Church. It does not follow from this that everyone who aspires to perfection should therefore seek to become a hermit. The eremitical life is a charism reserved for few. Most monks will remain in the cenobium. Nevertheless, the fact that the cenobitic life is safer and of wider appeal does not imply that the eremitical life is unsafe and has no appeal. The cenobium and the hermitage complete each other. If the cenobium disdains and repudiates the hermitage, it dooms itself to mediocrity. When the windows of the monastery no longer open out upon the vast horizons of the desert, the monastic community inevitably becomes immersed in vanity. All that is accidental, trivial, and accessory tends to assume a rank of high importance and to become the sole end of the monastic life. It is where monks have forgotten their potential destiny to solitude, that they allow themselves to run to seed in bickering about curiosities, or squandering their contemplative leisure in material cares.

This book should do something to remind us all of the monk's true destiny as a man of God. True, Paul Giustiniani lacks the freshness of Cassian and the Desert Fathers, the luminous simplicity of St. Benedict or St. Gregory, even more the sober enthusiasm of St. Bernard or the Greek Fathers. There is something in him of dryness which he contracted from the Stoics and from scholastic philosophy. But the genuine spirit of the desert is there, and the contemplation which brightens his pages is unmistakably true.

In closing this preface, I might observe that it is perhaps something altogether new and unusual for a book on an Italian hermit to appear, written by a

Benedictine in Luxemburg and prefaced by a Cistercian in the Southern United States. This joining together of Camaldoli, Monte Corona, Clervaux, and Gethsemani is surely significant. I dare to hope that it speaks very well for the union of the sons of St. Benedict with one another in our time—a union in prayer and deep charity and mutual understanding. If it be true, as I think it is, then our monasticism indeed has a function in the world. And it proclaims to all who will hear it the solemn affirmation of Christ who said: "Behold I am with you all days, even to the consummation of the world."[9]

—FR. M. LOUIS MERTON
Abbey of Gethsemani

---

[9] Matt. 28:19.

Introduction

I.

THE LIFE AND DOCTRINE
OF PAUL GIUSTINIANI

———————

Blessed Paul Giustiniani belongs among the men of God who, in the Italian Renaissance, steadfastly upheld the primacy of spiritual life. He was born in Venice in 1476 of a patrician family. Study absorbed him for many years, first in his own city, then in Padua at the University, and finally on the Island of Murano where he sought a seclusion entirely free of distraction. As a humanist and a follower of the Stoic doctrine, he renounced the pleasures of the flesh and turned increasingly towards God. Without forgetting Seneca and Cicero whose books were the source of his conversion, he nourished his soul on the Bible, the Fathers of the Church, the monastic writers of the Middle Ages, and the great Scholastics. In 1510 at the age of thirty-four he entered the hermitage of Camaldoli as a novice. A year and a half later, shortly after he had pronounced his vows, he was drawn to reform the whole Camaldolese Order. In 1520, after ten years of trouble and effort, he left the hermitage of Camaldoli to seek out a still more solitary life in absolute indigence. Disciples came to him with whom he founded the Company of the Hermits of St. Romuald, which continues to exist under the name of the Congregation of the Camaldolese hermits of Mount Corona. Ever since his death in 1528 his sons have called him *Blessed*.[1]

His many writings, which are almost entirely unpublished,[2] contain testimony of great historical value on many problems, as well as original and sound teaching. But in the midst of all other concerns, the core of Blessed Paul Giustiniani's teaching is his doctrine on the spiritual life in all its

---

[1] We follow the custom by using the title in this volume, though without any intention of anticipating the Church's judgment. On the history of this title, consult the texts collected by Dom N. Giustiniani in the Introduction to his edition of Blessed Paul Giustiniani's *Trattato dell' ubbidienza* (Padua, 1753).

[2] An inventory of Giustiniani's writings is found in Dom Leclercq's earlier book *Un humaniste ermite. Le bienheureux Paul Giustiniani.* (Rome, Ed. Camaldoli, 1951.) Appendix III, pp. 147-176. The references in this present volume are based on that inventory, which lists the titles of all the writings. The letters *F* and *Q* refer to the folio and quarto series of autograph manuscripts preserved in the Sacro Eremo Tuscolano of Frascati. The number following each letter is the number of the folio that contains the beginning of the quoted passage.

aspects. This constitutes the unity of his thought. This we must now examine, having completed the sketch of his life.[3] Blessed Paul was primarily a monk and a hermit: has spiritual doctrine, therefore, forms the core of his whole work; reflects his education; flows from the experiences of his life. This doctrine is an ample font that still quenches the thirst of the Congregation that he founded and developed. To pick out the main themes of his spiritual doctrine will in no way exhaust the treasure but will merely offer samples of its value.

Paul Giustiniani's writings contain the elements of a complete doctrine on the eremitic life. His open-minded attitude, wide culture, his philosophical, literary, and theological training that was typical of the highly developed civilization of his day —all this enabled him to view the whole panorama of diverse problems involved in the organization of an eremitic order. Because of thorough instruction in every field of knowledge he was familiar with examples and texts of classical times as well as those of the Middle Ages.[4] We could hardly claim that he has said everything on the subject of hermit life, but at least he has said something on its every aspect, considered all its problems, and given his opinion on them. However, he left no systematic treatise

---

[3] For a fuller account of Paul Giustiniani's life cf. *Un humaniste ermite*, op cit.

[4] Cf., Appendix I: The Sources of Blessed Paul Giustiniani, p. 201.

or fully developed presentation of his doctrine: his ideas are found scattered in a multitude of texts of heterogeneous types. Moreover, his chief purpose in writing was to develop his own thought, to express his fervor, or to stir up his friends' piety. His letters and exhortations are usually long and unsystematic. Hence the necessity—but also the difficulty —of gathering together these scattered elements and summarizing their contents. The synthesis we attempt here is almost wholly a mosaic of quotations translated and abridged.[5]

One of the principal sources will be the series of Rules written by Giustiniani: the original form written in 1516, the *Regula vitae eremiticae* of 1520,[6] finally the Constitutions of 1524 for the Company of Hermits of St. Romuald.[7] Even the first version contains the whole essence of Giustiniani's thought. In the revision of 1520 he merely devel-

---

[5] Passages that are translations, or in some cases summaries, of Blessed Giustiniani's texts, are placed between quotation marks. Because of the very nature of the sources we cannot always avoid repetitions and long-windedness.

[At the present time it is, unfortunately, impossible to obtain Giustiniani's original texts for direct translation from Latin or Italian into English. The quotations in the present volume are, therefore, translations of Dom Leclercq's French version.—Translator's note.]

[6] In footnotes this will be indicated by the abbrevation *RVE*. The Camaldoli edition of 1952 has been used.

[7] Concerning these texts see Appendix II of *Un humaniste ermite* on "Giustiniani as Lawgiver." op. cit., pp. 143-146.

oped and defined the same material, while adding detailed regulations concerning the cenobitic monasteries to which the hermitage of Camaldoli was attached. Thus he improved the organization of the community, but his fundamental ideas remained unchanged. The Constitution of 1524 was another recasting of the Rule of 1520 regarding the hermitage and reclusion. It retained the practical regulations, often virtually unmodified, but omitted the accompanying commentary. The successive Rules are, then, closely connected. The *Regula vitae eremiticae* is certainly the one most worthy of attention. It relies on earlier sources: some of its chapters consist of compilations of texts borrowed from the writings of St. Peter Damian, from the Camaldoli Constitutions of St. Rudolph (1080 and 1085), of Blessed Martin (1249 and 1253), and of Gerard the Prior (1278). But all these traditional elements were absorbed, selected, and assimilated by Giustiniani in such a personal way that they became truly his own and belong to his doctrine.

In general we need not take into account the chronology of the texts: while this would be the dominant factor in dealing with the author and his work from a historical point of view, it is quite secondary to the task of outlining his views on the eremitic life. The Company of Hermits of St. Romuald, though the ultimate form of his eremitic ideal, included almost all the details of teaching and organization already found in the Camaldoli hermitage. Giustiniani's descriptions of it set the pattern for his final work.[8] In this present book we are not concerned with the *coenobia* which continued to play an important role in the Rule of 1520. With these we shall not deal. The actual details on how life in the hermitages was regulated will be treated only in so far as they reveal lasting ideas.

Thus reduced to its simplest elements, Giustiniani's spiritual doctrine displays astonishing cohesion. His principal theme from which all else develops and which constantly appears in the texts is the basic premise of the whole hermit life: "Seek to live alone with God and to live for God alone." His teaching is perfectly balanced, presenting not only an ascetic doctrine or a mere psychology of the spiritual life, but also a real theology. Nor is it only an abstract theology: it is all centered upon and controlled by the mystery of Christ and the experiences of sacramental life. Moreover, far from being a purely personal or individual teaching its themes fit into the general pattern of man's redemption, while its texture is wholly formed by the mind of the Church.

In Giustiniani as theologian and as spiritual master we often catch glimpses of the humanist. His rich personality, his broad culture, his experience

---

[8] This fact has been clearly proved by the Camaldoli hermit, Dom S. Razzi, in his introduction to the Italian translation of the RVE published at Florence in 1575 under the title, *Regola della vita eremitica.*

of suffering enrich his texts with vibrant overtones of human interest. In several aspects his doctrine may seem excessively severe. To follow it completely requires an exceptional vocation and a particular grace which constitutes the eremitic charisma. However, the ideal of perfection that he presents, as well as at least some of his means to the end have universal value and can be helpful to any monk and to any Christian.

PART ONE

The Hermit's Vocation

II.

THE HERMIT'S ROLE
IN THE CHURCH

At the beginning of his first Rule Blessed Paul Giustiniani presents a general idea of the eremitic life. All his other texts develop the same notions. He first shows the place of the hermit within the whole Church. The Church's ultimate goal is the heavenly Jerusalem; every form of Christian life leads to that end. But there is one way of life that not only leads there but anticipates it. In the hermit life men are free of matters that often drive them away from heaven, and for that reason become like angels and live in the company of angels.[1]

To compare the eremitic life to other forms of Christian life, Giustiniani considers the Church in past centuries and in his own day. He notes first that there are diverse vocations within the unity of the Church.

[1] F A:3

"Some receive contemplation alone, that is, the soul's repose in God; others receive action only, which consists of toiling for God in external affairs; some are granted now one, then the other: contemplation for a time and action for a time, but never both together."[2]

Another fact, therefore, becomes self-evident: within the unity of Christian life there are many states of life differing in form and activity, but all animated by the same spirit, that divine life bestowed and communicated by Jesus Christ through His Church. On one common foundation of Christian duty is erected the threefold structure of *christiana vita, religiosa vita,* and *eremitica vita.* Each transcends the other: the second and the third are added to the first and must never depart from it. Before being a religious and in order to be one, a man must first be a Christian. Before being a hermit and in order to be one, a man must first be a Christian—truly be a Christian in reality and not only by name.[3] The holiness which belongs to every state of life is possible because they all share in the same life of Christ within the one holy Church. Without the faith and the practice of Christian duties, without submission to the Church, no way of life, however sublime it may appear, can possibly lead to salvation.

The states of life that *do* lead to salvation, since

---

[2] Q II:24.   [3] Q II:146.

they differ, have different values. But before emphasizing the degrees of perfection characteristic of each, we must recall that the personal perfection of every Christian depends primarily on his faithful response to his own vocation, whatever it may be.

"It is not the same to speak of men and of their state of life. When we say that religious life is more perfect than secular life, we compare one state of life to another state of life. But we do not mean that every religious is more perfect than all seculars. For we are sure that in a less perfect state of life there are men more perfect than those who live in a more perfect state. We believe that many married persons are more perfect than some who are widowed, and yet the state of widowhood is superior to that of marriage."[4]

What, then, is the place of hermit life among the various Christian vocations? It is one form of the religious state and therefore differs basically from secular life. Its essential excellence stems not from solitude for its own sake, but from the fact that it is a *religious* life. A man may be solitary without being a religious, and consequently, without following a higher state of life. In Giustiniani's time there were two kinds of Christians leading a secular life in the world: men immersed in tasks of an active life, living with their families and moving in society; then again other men who were living as hermits

[4] Q III:191.

without actually being such. As their way of life was not backed by the authority of the Church it was fraught with danger. The Fathers and the Councils of the Church are unanimous in maintaining that religious life, in comparison with secular life, is a surer way of reaching heaven.[5] Religious life itself comprises two general forms: active and contemplative. Active life is the religious life as led in communities other than hermitages. To accept such a definition we must remember the historical fact that in Giustiniani's time the monasteries were centres of active life. They were generally situated in cities where the monks were busy with the education of children, with preaching, with parish ministry, and other occupations outside the sphere of the religious life itself. Hence the conviction that Giustiniani never ceased to hold throughout his life and which in his time was indeed valid: contemplation requires the hermit life and is synonymous with it. These notions and distinctions will become clarified as we examine the texts. The following passage introduces and summarizes the matter:

"We must consider religious life on the one hand, and secular life on the other hand; then contemplative life, and finally active life. . . . If we compare first religious life to secular life we can easily find that the holy Fathers and the Church

[5] Giustiniani has collected their evidence on this point. Cf. Q III:191.

itself have defined that religious life is more perfect
and safer. To differ from their opinion would be not
only imprudent, but impious. . . . If now we wish
to compare active and contemplative life, we may
be sure that, in spite of all the controversy on this
subject, the final word is still Our Lord's promise:
'Mary has chosen the better part and it shall not be
taken away from her.'[6] As to activity, there is no
doubt that works of spiritual mercy, as they are
commonly called, should be preferred to all works
of corporal mercy. Thus in the secular state, among
the various ways of life it is more perfect to be
occupied in spiritual affairs than in corporal affairs.
Nevertheless this state of life is still very imperfect,
principally because the secular state in itself is a
great obstacle to the works of spiritual mercy. Similarly in the religious state: those who practise the
works of corporal mercy are in a state of perfection,
but their works are imperfect, especially because
such works hinder the perfection of their state.
Whence I conclude that pure contemplative life
would be most perfect, if our fragile nature were
capable of it. But since the human mind, particularly in those who have lived too long in a worldly
way, cannot remain always in a state of contemplation, the perfect life is found among those who, in
the religious state, practice contemplation as much
as possible and who, during the intervals when they

---

[6] Luke 10:42.

descend from their lofty heights, perform works of spiritual mercy."[7]

Such is the hermit's way of life. Because it is a form of religious life, it is quite distinct from all secular life, whether the latter be solitary or not. Its essential value derives, not from its particular form, but from the fact that it is a state of life approved by the Church. Like all forms of religious life, it requires three inseparable elements: the vows, a rule approved by the Church, and government by superiors whose authority is sanctioned by the rule and whom all must obey. Giustiniani often had to insist upon these three elements, as he reacted against the defects of what he called "secular hermits." At almost all times there have been Christians who have renounced worldly activity, though they do not wish and often are not able to lead a life determined by a rule. Some of them have attained sanctity in this path: in the first days of Oriental monasticism, for instance, various ascetics achieved great virtue in spite of and sometimes by means of very eccentric behavior. In more recent times Benedict Joseph Labre has demonstrated that it is possible to become a saint without belonging to any "state of perfection."[8] But these instances were

---

[7] Q II:178.

[8] This vagabond hermit's particular form of sanctity is well described in Dom P. Doyère's book, *Saint Benoît-Joseph Labre, ermite pèlerin, 1748-1783*. (Paris, 1948.)

always considered exceptions. Monastic reformers and lawgivers warned against the dangers of any solitary life that lacked the safeguard of a rule and a lawful superior. There were solitaries of this kind in Giustiniani's day and he often exhorted them to enter religious life. In his first Rule he declared his intention of making a place for them in the Church.

"Eremitic life was of old considered the highest glory of Christian life and of the religious state; but in our day it has declined even more than other forms of religious life and has almost disappeared. In fact only the twenty or more Camaldolese hermits who follow the Rule of St. Benedict and their own legal constitutions are truly leading a religious life as hermits. All others who live in solitude or who in any way enjoy the title of "hermits" are in face neither hermits nor religious, because they lack the first requisites of religious life: they pronounce no vows of religion, profess no approved rule, do not obey a superior. Their deplorable conduct must be censured, for they do not serve God, but just their own desires, contravening the sacred canons."[9]

The vows of religion are important in more than one respect: they admit a Christian to a state of life approved by the Church; they stamp his whole existence with the seal of obedience, the only escape from illusion; they constitute a noble act of the virtue of religion, a consecration that enhances the

---

[9] F A:3. Unpublished prologue to the Rule of 1516.

value and increases the merit of whatever acts of virtue a Christian voluntarily performs.

"Even if one who has not taken the vows observes poverty, chastity, and obedience perfectly, even if he seems to proceed along an arduous path, nevertheless he cannot acquire the richer merit of religious life. The Church teaches through her saints that all good works become better and more meritorious when offered to God by a vow, particularly a solemn public vow. To make a vow is an act of adoration, of the worship due to God alone, the worship most pleasing to Him, because it raises all subsequent actions to a sublime level of perfection." Whoever makes a vow offers God not only his actions but himself. He consecrates to the Lord once and for all not only the proper use of liberty, but that whole liberty itself. He enters an entirely new relationship with the Lord, so that the vows truly resemble a second baptism.[10]

But religious life has two principal forms: active and contemplative. We must first define them clearly in order that we may grasp the distinction and the connection between them.

"By 'contemplative life' I do not mean the future life, the one true life of perfect contemplation in which we shall see God and enjoy perpetual bliss. Nor do I mean the spiritual ecstasy that is occasion-

---

[10] Q II:155. This text summarizes traditional theology regarding the vows of religion.

ally granted during this earthly life to certain souls of great perfection, a sort of vision of divine truths, bestowed as a special grace in a way that transcends the usual limitations of human nature. I refer instead to the manner of life of those who have renounced all temporal and spiritual activity in order to heed only God and themselves—*sibi soli et Deo vacat.* They strive, as constantly as human frailty permits, to reach God by reading holy books, by meditating on the eternal truths, and by persisting in prayer. By 'active life' I do not refer to the state of those who spend their time on the vanities of the world or on secular business, but I mean a way of life which makes room for the duties of taking care of other souls as well as various other activities that pious men may undertake for the honor and the service of religion."[11]

In comparing these two forms of religious life, the active and the contemplative, we must judge each by the value of its distinctive traits. "We can easily collect texts by various doctors of the Church proving that total contemplative life (*total,* that is, in so far as human frailty permits) is more perfect, since its one aim is to love and to know God which is the most perfect life and at the same time most useful to other men, even though its usefulness is not apparent. . . . According to the doctrine of St. Thomas who, in a way, prefers active to contem-

---

[11] Q I:41.

plative religious life, there are two kinds of actions in religious life, the first antecedent to contemplation, the second springing from the experience of contemplation. Now even those who somewhat prefer action to contemplation agree that the action which precedes contemplation is less perfect than contemplation itself. The action proceeding from contemplation is likewise less perfect than contemplation itself. I personally have always held the opinion that both forms of action are less perfect than contemplation. Regarding action which leads to contemplation there is no doubt. A man whose action proceeds from contemplation generally does not undertake action as if he were climbing to a higher level, but rather he goes to a lower level in order to offer services necessary to his neighbor and unobtainable from others. To turn from God's love and the loving of God (which is contemplation) to the process of loving one's neighbor is not an upward but a downward movement. We do not love God for the sake of our neighbor, but our neighbor for the sake of God. . . . If our neighbor needs help in order to save his soul, and if there be none other to care for him, we may, without risking our own salvation, consent to lose something of our perfection, or some portion of superfluous consolation in order that we may attend to his urgent needs. Similarly the Fathers of the Church teach that Christians, and priests in particular, have no right to take flight and hide in times of persecution if this deprives the Christian people of necessary means of salvation. They should rather stay and face the risks. So I believe that when others are available, contemplatives may be excused from good works for the benefit of their neighbors. But if there is a lack of persons to offer the services necessary to their neighbors' salvation, then the contemplatives should interrupt and relinquish their lives of contemplation to accept a life that is less perfect but more necessary. They do not then advance upward, but stoop downward. They should not do this through mere love of neighbor, for they should never remove their attention from love of God in order to attend lovingly to their neighbors. I say that their motive should not be natural love of neighbor, but primarily love of God and service of God through service of neighbor. . . . At the present time those who practice works of spiritual mercy on behalf of their neighbors, far from being wanting are most plentiful."[12]

An entirely contemplative life is, then, legitimate. Objectively it represents the highest level of perfection. In Giustiniani's time this coincided with eremitic life, being found only in hermitages. He maintained that these were intended by Providence to encourage and preserve that perfect life in the Church. In his general introduction to the 1520 edition of the Rule he traced the general outline of

_____

[12] Q II:178.

monastic history in order to situate the Camaldoli hermit life in its proper background.

"Among the numerous forms of monastic life only two are admirable and pleasing to God: the cenobitic and the eremitic life. Both originated in the East in the blessed days of the early Fathers, the first founded by St. Anthony, the second by St. Paul. According to St. Jerome, St. Paul was the first to lead the solitary life in the desert, while Anthony was the first to train disciples in monastic life. As leader and originator of hermit life, Paul must be forever honored as the first hermit. Anthony is acknowledged as founder of community life because he was the first to teach many monks to live together in a common dwelling, sharing the wherewithal for sustaining their human frailty. These monks, therefore, were called 'cenobites' which means 'living in community.' Anthony was likewise the first to receive the title of *abbot*, that is, *father* of many brothers living together.

"In the West, the establishment of monastic life, as well as many other things related to Christian faith, occurred only much later. There too, however, as in the East, it claims two equally renowned and holy founders: Benedict and Romuald. For the holy Benedict is called patriarch of Western cenobites, not because that life was unknown previously, but because he was the first in the Western Church to draw up the rules of community life. And though he himself, as St. Gregory relates, adopted the hermit life at the beginning of his conversion when he spent three years in a little cave unknown to all men but the monk Romanus, yet later he changed to cenobitic life. As leader and founder of the cenobitic institution he wrote his rule of life for cenobites alone, disregarding other kinds of monks. And though he always preferred what St. Gregory called 'the place of his cherished solitude' yet for the benefit of the majority, he lived with the community as father and abbot of many monks at his Monastery of Monte Cassino until his happy and glorious departure to Christ.

"In the meantime, while hermit life doubtless claimed adherents in the Western Church, yet for a time no one actually organized it. Its first founder was a man of wondrous holiness and admirable life, St. Romuald. He was the first to transmit to his contemporaries and to bequeath to future generations the constitutions and rules of eremitic life, not in written form, but by the example of his life and teaching. In this he imitated Christ, our Lord, who did not put into written form the ideal that He practiced and taught, but left it to others to write down afterwards. St. Romuald's biographer, St. Peter Damian, tells us that the holy Romuald first led a cenobitic life for three years in the then famous monastery of Classe in Ravenna. But when he became more eager for greater perfection he transferred to the hermit life and, like St. Paul the Hermit, he persevered in it faithfully until death . . . He founded many hermitages in different regions not only in Italy but beyond the Alps and overseas. Countless men flocked to him from every direction and he trained them in the hermit life. Even within his own lifetime several of his disciples achieved the palm of martyrdom.

"But if we seek the origin of these two modes of life in more remote antiquity, we find that in the Old Testament, Elias practiced the solitary way of life, while his disciple, Eliseus, in company with many followers, organized community life. Whoever ponders on these incidents will understand that these two modes of monastic sanctity were not invented by men but were given to the human race by God, who governs all things wisely, who loves human beings supremely, and who even in Old Testament days providentially sent Elias and Eliseus to show these two modes of religious life to the men whom He wished to save. These are the two paths by which men may easily arrive at eternal bliss. Later when the Gospel had been proclaimed, the same two paths were more clearly and openly marked out in the East by St. Paul and St. Anthony, in the West by St. Benedict and St. Romuald. With their help men could journey on these two royal roads and thus safely reach the unutterable delights of the heavenly Jerusalem, the place prepared for those who fear and love God. And if we examine the origin and progress of these two modes of life, we can easily perceive that they are like two sisters showing a close resemblance, though wearing different clothing. Moreover, if we consider carefully not only their origin, but also their respective characteristics, it becomes evident that they are linked by such a close relationship and intimate bond that the fullness of cenobitic life is impossible without some participation in the hermit life, and the latter cannot be perfect without some form of support from the cenobites. It is undeniable that anyone who has any experience of either one or the other life knows that each needs the help of the other, and that both have many important features in common. For truly a monk—if we think of the real meaning of the word—is 'one who lives in solitude.'[13] But the word is rightly applied to those who live together in a monastery, as well as to the hermits dwelling in the same solitude and following the same vocation. The word *monastery* has come to mean the home of a community living together. Both the hermit and the cenobite are known as solitaries because, in so far as human weakness permits, they withdraw from the exterior and the interior multitude, that is, they remove themselves externally from the throngs of other men whose lives

---

[13] *Monk* is from the Greek *monachos*, from *monos: alone.*

differ from theirs. At the same time, by interior discipline and unceasing practice of virtue, they strive to expel from their soul the many passions and impulses disturbing it, in order that divine love alone might dwell in their hearts. Therefore, one who wishes to live without companions cannot be more truly called a *monk* on that account than one who, even though he shares the company of others as a way of more perfectly devoting himself to God alone, yet truly escapes both physically and spiritually from the common throngs. It matters not if he practice his way of life with many brothers in a monastery or if he dwell alone in a hermitage. . . .

"When the cenobites learn of the rules of hermit life, they may either persevere humbly in their own life, while applying some elements of the eremitic ideal within their own monastery, or else they may transfer from the monastery to the hermitage, from their battle station in the ranks of the army to a post of single combat, from a perfect way of life to a more perfect way of life. This is not forbidden in any community rule nor by any pronouncement of St. Benedict. More than once he declared that those most ardent in the quest of perfection might well advance from the gentle initiation of cenobitic life to the robust maturity of the hermit's way. Thus progress takes place from the good to the better, from one virtue to another, by a direct path of ascent towards the summit which all should crave.

On the other hand when hermits read the Rule governing cenobites, they should blush for shame and amend their ways if they perceive that they, who are bound to the higher and nobler duties of the eremitic life, do not attain even the full perfection proper to the lower and easier precepts of cenobitic life. Thus they can see more clearly what utter purity of life and integral perfection of all virtue is expected of them, if already the discipline of cenobitic life is a perfection. To fall short of *that* ideal would be shameful on the part of those whose profession (if they are true hermits) binds them to a still stricter and more excellent discipline. . . .

"But especially in our day it is important that the Rule and the practices of eremitic life be made known, in particular to those who seek to serve God. . . . For in other times all who decided to lead monastic life sought out solitary places. The Councils and the holy canons forbade monks to live in cities or even to enter them. But now the monks have come down from their lofty solitude and have mingled with the worldly throngs of city streets, either because they had to take refuge from the disturbances caused by wars or because they wished to help Christians in secular life to save their souls. They have exchanged the paradise of all delight for a wretched prison. But it has come about now that city-dwellers are more upset by wars than those inhabiting the deserts, while the conduct of monks no longer proves helpful in the salvation of laymen. . . . It is time, therefore, for the monks to leave the monasteries located within city walls and to seek once more the greater freedom of remote solitudes."[14]

---

[14] RVE f.II-V.

III.

CHRIST'S CALL

The hermit life, then, does exist and in Giustiniani's time it was the refuge of contemplatives. But who can be admitted to it? Being more perfect and more difficult than any other life, the vocation to it must be all the more evident.

There must be a vocation. To recognize it, we must first know what it is not. The illusion of false vocations is by no means unreal.

"Some men who experience neither spiritual devotion nor desire to reform their lives nor zeal for God's glory, nevertheless wish to enter religious life. And why? Because they hope that religious life will give them some particular advantage which they prize: perhaps physical rest or leisure for reading and study. In some cases they want to be fed and clothed and cared for in sickness and old age. Sometimes the motive is vanity—the wish to be admired, to acquire a reputation for virtue, to live on a higher plane than they can reach as laymen. But such desires must be discouraged. A candidate showing such dispositions must be reminded of the Sage's advice: 'My son, if you enter God's service prepare your soul, not for delights, honor, or rank, but for temptation.' We must point out, as St. Benedict directs, how many hard and arduous trials await those who seek to follow Christ. Such warnings will cause these aspirants either to refrain from entering religious life, or to correct their motives. Christ did the same when a certain man promised to follow Him everywhere. Jesus answered: 'The foxes have holes, and the birds of the air nests; but the Son of man hath not where to lay his head.'[1] It was as if he said to that man: 'You say that you will follow me, but perhaps you are hoping for an easier life or seeking fame and a high position in the world. Be assured that you will be disappointed.' I assure you that Jesus Christ provides for His followers not ease but trouble; not honor but contempt, insults, dishonor, calumny; not advancement, but subjection. In God's service even authority means service and subjection.

"If anyone seek to enter religion to be served rather than to serve, to relax rather than to become wearied, he should be told: 'Depart, my son, depart. You seek rest in religious life? You will find anxi-

[1] Luke 9:58.

ety. You seek to be praised, admired as good and holy? You will be blamed and insulted; more often than not even your good deeds will be repaid with scorn. You seek high rank? I tell you that to enter religious life means to live in constant slavery, perpetual subjection. Even if you are promoted to a post of authority, the yoke will become still heavier, for you will be the servant of servants."[2]

To enter religious life means to follow Christ—Christ alone.

"St. Dominic and St. Francis were men subject to error. But Christ was the Son of God: it is Him alone they followed. We truly imitate Dominic and Francis, Augustine and Benedict, when we follow Christ, for they strove only to imitate Him. Christ is the true leader, the way and the goal. With Francis and Dominic and all Christ's followers let us run along the fragrant path, setting our feet in His footsteps. Let us run towards Christ Himself, not towards the holy founders. Christ is the target at which all the arrows of our desire should be aimed. Dominic and Francis shot their arrows towards that mark; let us shoot ours to the same spot. This in nowise lessens the respect due to these saints: we simply wish to follow the leader whom they followed. St. Francis' humility and poverty only teach us to follow the humble and poor Christ. Do the Rules of St. Dominic, St. Benedict, or St. Augustine

---

[2] F VII:28 and 138.

have any other purpose but to turn us towards Christ? They show the way for us to follow Christ; they do not offer themselves as leaders. There is only one leader, for them as for us.

"Let our Rule of life be the life of Christ; let our written rule be the Gospel, to which we must always cling, taking care never to stray from Christ's own rules. There lies true religious life, the norm of all perfection. What is in the Rules of St. Dominic or of St. Francis that is not found in the Gospel? Since we are Christians, let us renew ourselves, as by a new baptism. Let us resolve to follow Christ alone. What St. Paul told the Corinthians applies to us. Did Dominic and Francis redeem us in their blood? Have we been clothed in the spirit of Dominic or Francis? By no means. Christ is the font of living water; all these saints are but tributary streams. Let us drink from the source itself. Let us journey along the royal road, following, as they did, the One who has called us."[3]

A vocation then is not an invitation like those issued by the world. It is a call from the Lord, an invitation that must be received humbly, without presumption. For if Jesus Himself does not supply the means of complying with His demands, man is powerless to do so. Christ calls us and He attracts us. When a man hears that voice, he should not only answer: "Guide me, lead me, teach me how to

---

[3] F + :96.

follow you." But he should also plead, like the bride of the Canticles: "Draw me. *Trahe me*, that is: Force me, compel me to walk after you. For I cannot follow you of my own accord. On the contrary, even if you call me, you must also show me the path: if you do not draw me, if you do not use your strength, I shall never succeed in following you."

A vocation is a grace of preference; it implies a choice on God's side; man's role is only to consent. " 'You have not chosen me, but I have chosen you,' said the Lord.[4] It is certain that man cannot enter religious life if God has not chosen him for it. The call to follow Christ must come from God, not from oneself. God chooses whom He will; those He chooses, He calls. But all do not answer the divine call. Some say: 'I have bought a farm, and I must needs go out and see it.'[5] What really is required? God must draw us. 'No man can come to me, except the Father, who hath sent me, draw him.'[6] God must force us to leave the world and to partake of the feast of religious life at Christ's table, to take up the cross and to follow Him. Do we not learn that Lot refused to leave Sodom, though invited by angels? He had to be forced. Does not Scripture say: 'The angels pressed him . . . and as he lingered, they took his hand. . . . And they brought him forth, and set him without the city.'[7] The Lord must speak to us

---

[4] John 15:16.   [5] Luke 14:18.   [6] John 6:44.
[7] Gen. 19:15-17.

with authority; He must overcome our weakness and resistance, as well as the attractions of the world. He must force us to follow Him. He tells us that we do not follow Him because we choose Him, but because He chooses us. If human choice does not coincide with God's choice it is worth nothing. If God has not called you, chosen you, drawn you to religious life, do not imagine that human judgment or human prudence or human exhortation can have any effect."

But how will God utter His call? "He calls His servants to religious life in many ways: some by an inner inspiration, some by the silent example of other men, some by human exhortations, some by prosperity, others by adversity. But however the call comes, blessed is he who is not deaf to the divine vocation."[8] Often God's call sounds in the soul by the voice of Holy Scripture. It rouses the soul and kindles a desire that is the clearest sign of vocation. "God called you when He put in your heart the desire to leave the world and to take refuge in poverty and nakedness, bearing the yoke of Christ. Such aspirations cannot rise from human weakness. . . . If you have heard this call, do not be deaf to it and do not refuse to answer. Otherwise we may fear that you will have no right to divine mercy at the Last Judgment. Those who were not called, who were not privileged to feel such a desire,

[8] F VII:28 and 138.

will all have an excuse. But you whom divine grace deigned to rouse from your lethargic sleep, and opened your eyes to eternal truth, you have been called to undertake religious life. Your desire is the gesture of putting your hand to the plow: do not look backwards."[9]

A vocation is imperative. It respects liberty but creates an obligation. When the Lord has uttered His call, He must be followed without delay. "One need not wander about visiting every religious house in search of the one place where God can be served in perfect serenity. No need to expect some marvellous sign or divine miracle to point out the way. You must seek God, that is, hasten to meet Him, not sit back with arms crossed expecting His coming. You must act decisively, set out without fearing criticism, run the risk of being misunderstood by good men, even risk scandalizing evil men. For in proportion as good men are edified by a holy way of life, so are bad men scandalized by it. Frequently even, the more perfect a way of life is, the more sinners blush and are abashed to see others correct their vices, and the worse are the insults and calumnies they utter against it. But in the Gospel our Lord, when speaking of the Pharisees, taught us to pay no attention to their opinions. . . . St. Paul said likewise that the good odor of Christ is an odor of life for some men and of death for others."[10]

---

[9] F VII:87. [10] Q IV:345.

A man who has begun to follow Christ should not be divided between Christ and the world. Having put his hand to the plough, he should not look back. "In the first fervor of conversion, he should abandon and utterly despise all worldly things, all obstacles to his free and joyful following of Christ. If he looks backward towards those whom he has left at home, if he is anxious about any worldly affairs, then he will be all the less able later to restrain his desires to see, to help, to console those whom he has left behind. How many there are who have been inspired by Christ to follow Him and to become religious, but who first wish to provide their families, not only with the necessities of life, but with superfluities. They want to find husbands for their nieces and wives for their nephews! Of course they wish to become religious, but they want to stay in their own region, enter a monastery where they will be allowed to write often to their parents and their nephews, see them, and receive their visits. Receive visits, yes indeed! Why, they even want to go and visit them in their own homes and dine with them!"

A vocation demands courageous separation. He who wishes to become a religious should not immediately tell his plan to his family; his father, mother, brothers and sisters, for he can expect from them many hindrances and difficulties. They may induce him to change his mind. Let him rather think of these words of the Lord: "No one who looks behind him, when he has once put his hand to the plough, is fitted for the Kingdom of God."[11] "Fearing lest he be hampered, let him abandon the world and enter religious life without stirring up countless obstacles by warning his relatives. Soon enough to let them know once the thing has been done."[12]

As a vocation is a gift from God, it confers the required strength. God is wise and if He really calls a Christian to the life of solitude, He gives also whatever aptitudes and health are necessary. "If I saw a doctor buying a sickly slave to serve him, I would think that the doctor knew about the illness and could cure the slave so that he would be able to serve his master. Similarly if God calls you to the solitary religious life, I think that you must have the necessary health, or if you lack it, God will give you strength to bear the hardships of the life. According to the Fathers of the Church, if the soul is weak, God gives whatever help is needed through the practices of religious life, by the good example and exhortations received there which, with divine grace, can strengthen the weak. Naturally the same principle applies to physical weakness. Experience indeed proves it. Among many others, I have seen a man enter eremitic life at forty years of age, so incapable of fasting that he had never fasted for even one day in his whole life, not even on Good Friday, because he was sure that he could not do so.

---

[11] Luke 9:62.   [12] F VII:28 and 138.

Either he *could* do it, but thought he could not, or being really unable to do it previously, he received the necessary strength from God: in any case I have seen him observe perfectly, without any impairment of health, all the fasts and abstinences of the Camaldolese Hermitage: the daily fast from September thirteenth to Easter, the Lenten fast twice a year (with three days a week on bread and water), the simple fast of bread, water, and fruit on Fridays throughout the year, as well as other abstinences. He himself was amazed by it!

"Recently a man came to me who had been a doctor in secular life and who was, or appeared to be, of such delicate health that, though he tried his best to observe Lent, he hardly ever could persevere to the end: fasting seemed extremely difficult for him. Now that he has become a religious he fasts even more strictly than the common rule requires and it seems nothing to him. On the contrary, he feels as if he were leading a pampered life and he is healthier and stronger than ever before. But why speak only of the example of others? *"Iste pauper clamavit et Dominus exaudivit eum."*[13] I myself lived a secular life for thirty-four years and from the age of twenty until the age of thirty-three I suffered a serious illness almost every year. Even when I was well, the price of health was very high. There was almost nothing that I could eat: no

13 Ps. 33:7.

salads, salted food, tart fruits, vegetables, oil, etc. The slightest excess in quality or quantity, the slightest change in the time of my meals had a distressed effect. If I fasted, I could not sleep. To conceal nothing of my weakness, I even considered myself so weak and incapable of keeping Lent that I thought I committed no sin by not observing it. If by chance I wished to keep the Lenten fast all my relatives objected and caused me qualms of conscience, saying that I was trying to become ill by doing what experience had proved to be beyond my strength. In short, I was constantly sick and everyone supposed that I had no more than two years to live. Well the truth is that since my conversion to religious life I have always observed, as a very minimum, all the fasts of the Camaldoli Hermitage without any ill effects. Not only 'without ill effects,' but I really am cured and in much better health. Nothing in our prescribed diet disagrees with me. To delay or advance the time for eating does not trouble me. I feel no pain in my stomach or my head. I have as much sleep as my body needs. In fact I sometimes have the impression that these twelve or thirteen years of eremitic life have not aged me, but have actually rejuvenated me by many years."

"It would be presumptuous to expect extraordinary help from God. That He confers very rarely. But the help I mention has been given to many and it is quite understandable. If a man chooses an approved rule and a life that others are also leading, he is praiseworthy if he trust in God. The Lord does not abandon those who trust Him. *'Quis confisus est in Domino, et Dominus dereliquit eum?'* As long as we trust ourselves, as long as we gauge our strength by the standard of human prudence which is vain and false, we are always frail, helpless, and timid. But if we commend ourselves into God's hands, we shall straightway feel strong and fearless."[14]

---

[14] Q II:178.

IV.

WORDLESS PREACHING

The hermit life exists in the Church and some Christians are called to it. But at the same time that we note these two facts a question arises in our mind. What is the hermit's role? Sometimes the question is put in the form of an objection: "It is often believed that within the whole framework of Christian life the solitary life is either entirely useless or is the least useful organ of the mystical body of the Holy Catholic Church. It is almost a current belief that a hermit can be useful only to himself. Therefore, some condemn that way of life or retire from it, fearing the fate of the servant who hid the talent entrusted him instead of making it bear fruit."[1]

This objection, while easy to formulate, is difficult to refute. To do so we must recall certain

---

[1] Q IV bis:103.

principles. "Christians should seek their neighbors' salvation and God's glory, but in different ways. Each man, by carrying on his own proper work and purpose, without usurping the role of others, should seek God's glory and, in view of God's glory, his neighbor's salvation. It would be ridiculous and regrettable if one member of the body of which Christ is head, were to try to take on the functions of all the other members. You, who are hermits, who are not bishops or pastors, but just sheep of the flock, you should seek God's glory and your neighbors' salvation, not by restless activity, but by prayer and entreaty, for this is the hermit's proper role. Why should you rashly try to swing your scythe in another man's field? Why do you try to do another's duty? That is not your task. It is not for you to become immersed in the turmoil of worldly affairs. Not for that purpose did God intend that you be born, that you grow up with a desire for solitude, and be converted to His service. It was to allow you leisure that you might pray assiduously: for that alone He attracted you to Himself, removed you, as it were evicted you from the realm of worldly concerns."[2]

In the life of every Christian and of every religious, fruitfulness depends upon each one's fidelity to his personal vocation. "Like all who follow Christ, the hermit has heard the invitation which the

[2] Q III:4ʳ.

Lord issues in the Gospel: 'Going, preach, saying: the Kingdom of heaven is at hand.' "[3] To follow Christ is to preach the kingdom of heaven. What truly does it mean *to preach the kingdom of heaven?* It means to scorn the kingdom of the world. How then does one preach the kingdom of heaven? Oh surely, surely the kingdom of heaven is eloquently preached by all who can say with Christ: 'My kingdom is not of this world.'[4] He who with all his heart truly renounces the pleasures and honors and rank of this world proclaims the Kingdom of God more than if he preached it in a thousand languages, but did not teach it in his life. He shouts out not only with his mouth but with all his members: 'I have no permanent dwelling in this world. Here I wish neither father, mother, friend, nor relatives because I look forward to another kingdom in heaven, a kingdom not built by human hands. I long for, I hope for, I hasten towards the kingdom of heaven, the kingdom of God. This kingdom is preached by any man who testifies that this mortal life is a pilgrimage towards the land of our true home, any man who proves that this earth is no true home, that the place of our real home is the celestial land.

"The kingdom of God was proclaimed by the Apostles, by the martyrs, the virgins, the Fathers of the Church, and the hermits. The Apostles

---

[3] Matt. 10:7.   [4] John 18:36.

preached by speaking and by performing miracles in the name of Jesus. The martyrs preached by joyfully facing death and torture to confess that they longed for the kingdom of heaven. The virgins preached by rejecting earthly pleasure and carnal passion in exchange for the chaste delights of heaven. The doctors preached in defending the truth by dint of ceaseless study and in announcing the future judgment, the eternal bliss of Christ's servants, and the perpetual punishment of those who love this world. The hermits of old preached by their total renouncement, by giving up all things, by fleeing from all joy, honor, worldly position. They, it is evident, proclaimed the kingdom of heaven more by deeds than by words, through their whole life, with their whole self.

"For to leave one's country, wealth, honor, and position in order to go and live in the desert, poor and despised, to practice the eremitical austerities in eating and drinking, to sleep on the bare ground, to wear a rough habit, and to endure all the other rigors of eremitic life: what is all this but a cry to worldlings: 'how foolish and how blind you are—intoxicated by worldly pleasure and honor, you forget the delights of heaven, the glories of the celestial realm. Do you think we are so foolish as to miss reaching a better life because we refuse to renounce the pleasures that prevent our arriving there? We sacrifice voluntarily all that causes pleasure in this life because the gaze of our soul is ever fixed on the kingdom of heaven. God's kingdom is more easily accessible to those who more truly despise the world and accept the cross of Christ, prepared to crucify all the concupiscences and their very selves with Christ. I claim that in our time there is no truer nor more effective way to proclaim the kingdom of God than to become a religious. Do you not believe that men who know you and consider you wise and prudent, when they see you leave your country, your house and your abundant possessions will say: 'surely that prudent, educated, intelligent man would not abandon all that wealth, were he not sure that after this life he would receive a nobler and dearer homeland, a grander house, more substantial possessions, keener pleasures, higher honors, a mightier position.' So though your tongue be mute, your whole life and all your actions, your very person proclaim the kingdom of God. . . . He who preaches the kingdom of God in the way most calculated to help his neighbor is the man who renounces the most wealth, honor, and dignity. He most clearly shows how wretched is all else compared to the kingdom of heaven."[5]

From this point of view religious profession acquires a new value. The vows are a consecration to God, but they are also an effective example because they are a public testimony.

"To teach or to correct others or to perform any

---

[5] F VII:28 and 138.

other spiritual works of mercy are fruitless tasks if the teacher or reformer does not first himself achieve fully what he urges on others. Nor can he help his neighbors if his own reform be merely interior, for human minds cannot perceive what is hidden in another man's heart. The man who would be useful to others must practice openly and outwardly what he wants to teach. Scripture says: 'Coepit Jesus facere et docere!'[6] . . . Therefore the very act of leaving and despising all worldly things in order to devote oneself to God and to religious life by a public act of profession, that act by itself is a spiritual work of mercy that is more perfect, more pleasing to God, and more fruitful for others than all that a man could do throughout his whole life while remaining in the secular state. A man remaining in the world may help one particular neighbor to correct one vice, or he may train another in one virtue, but if he openly renounce all vice and all occasion of vice, if he embraces the state of life that best fosters virtue, if he enlists forever as a humble servant of God, then he offers the strongest sermon on virtue, the strongest repudiation of vice, the strongest explanation of what it means to despise the world and to love and serve God. By a single deed he preaches on every virtue and arouses hatred of every sin. This lesson reaches not only the ten or a hundred persons whom he

---

[6] Act. I:1.

knows personally, but it extends to more than a thousand, to all the living and to all who will come after him and to whom he may point out as clearly as he can the path they should follow in fleeing from sin, loving virtue, and seeking wholeheartedly their salvation and God's glory."[7]

The hermit's way of serving his neighbor is to remain true to his vocation as a hermit. His very responsibility towards his neighbor obliges him to *be* perfectly what he should be. "Woe to us if we provide no edification to those who expect it of us, if the perfection of our life does not encourage the hesitant and allure the seekers. . . . For men expect more from religious and priests than from laymen. Of those who have left all things and have 'become eunuchs' for the sake of the kingdom of heaven, of the followers of the Lord, much more is demanded than of those who try to practice the Christian faith in the midst of marriage and possessions. And we above all who, with God's help, have embraced the solitary life which is so perfect, so sublime, so very austere, we must offer only what is great and only what is perfect. Woe to us if those who seek the Lord must blush for our conduct! Woe to us if our light does not shine before men so that, seeing our good works, they may glorify the Father in heaven! Let us take care then that our good works and the radiance of our virtues, our existence before all

[7] Q II:178.

nations on this peak of the Appennines, may force ever those who do not wish to know God to confess that to serve Almighty God sincerely and in truth brings the only real happiness possible in this world."[8]

The more we strive for personal perfection, the more we help our neighbor. "Mary's leisure is not less fruitful than Martha's work. For that leisure is not inert, idle, and drowsy, (as happens all too often with prelates whose honors contribute more to their own relaxation than to the welfare of their subjects). Mary's leisure is busier than all work and it is as much more useful to herself and to others as action is more useful than talking, as giving an example is more useful than preaching. In this isolated leisure more help is given to oneself and to others than in absorbing work. And if I may quote the example of pagans, I believe that what was written of Cicero can truly be said of us: that in a short time of leisure he rendered greater service to his fellow citizens as well as to all posterity than by many years' work. . . . The soul at rest is more serene and free: therefore, a hidden life is better than public life. Active life reaches a high level, according to the opinion of the Peripatetics, if it succeeds even in moderating and restraining the passions, thus preventing their overstepping the bounds restraining them from vice and wickedness.

[8] Q IV:345.

The life of leisure, on the other hand, according
to the Stoics, accomplishes nothing unless it frees
men entirely from all their passions, leaving no
room for them, banishing them permanently."[9]

The fruitfulness of a life is measured less by immediate results than by the excellence of the being
to whom it is dedicated. A life wholly given to God
is more useful than a life divided between God and
what is not God. "The man most useful to the
human race is the one who can help the greatest
number of people in the most ways and for the
longest time, not in the physical but in the spiritual
sphere. He serves them not for this short life, but
for the future life. He points out a shorter and a
quicker path to the goal of all desire, eternal beati-
tude. Such is the case with the solitary. Matters of
the soul and eternal life are more important than
matters of the body and earthly life. Now there are
three ways of helping men spiritually: by teaching
and preaching, by the power of example, and by
imploring divine help in prayer and in other meritorious works. Teaching is accomplished by word
or by writing: these are similar, for what are words
but transient documents and what are writings but
persisting words? Men can give good example by
particular virtuous actions or by their whole manner of life. The third way of help is given by those
who think of others in their vocal or mental prayers,

---

[9] Q IV bis:252ᵛ.

or by those whose good works are so meritorious that for love of them, God grants His help to others besides themselves. Thus we read that God set Lot free for the love of Abraham, and did not do so because of Abraham's request, but because of his holy life. All these means of help are available to the solitary, who, other things being equal, is more useful to the human race than men who are not solitary."[10]

The contemplative helps his neighbor more than others, just as a subject who gains a prince's favor helps his family more than the man who tries to amass a fortune by working. A prince's patronage brings greater benefit at one stroke than all the exertions of many years. Imagine someone who knows nothing of the art of navigation but who wishes to cross the sea with his whole family: he will take better care of himself and all his family by trusting an expert sailor than by trying to steer the ship himself. Similarly he who knows that God is the reliable, wise, and infinitely good captain of the human race is more useful to himself and to all other men if he commits to God all care of himself and of his neighbor. He strives to acquire and retain the Lord's favor by appealing to Him incessantly."[11] Thus good deeds and prayer are the two ways that the solitary truly serves Christianity. But here is the ultimate explanation of this usefulness.

[10] Q IV bis:103.   [11] Q IV bis:128.

"In the Credo we say each day that we believe in the Communion of Saints. What do these few words imply? That all prayers and all good deeds, all the merits of all the saints are common to all Christ's good servants. . . . It is not I who thus explain these words, but the very learned Doctor, St. Thomas. Commenting on this article of the Creed, he says that all Christians are members of the body of which Jesus Christ is the head. And just as the food which the body receives is common to all the members, so the good accomplished in this body, of which the saints in heaven are also members, is common to all the other members, except those that break away from it of their own accord, or who are amputated by excommunication and thus are no longer able to receive its nourishment."[12]

To justify the hermit's way of life in the Church, Blessed Paul Giustiniani refers more often to the example offered *to* others, than to prayer *for* others. We might be surprised that after his strong presentation of the dogma of the Communion of Saints he does not give greater importance to the prayer of intercession. But we must admit that in this he follows the most authentic monastic tradition. He cannot be refuted from the theological point of view. He emphasizes the divine transcendence and the excellence of a life wholly centered on God. Because God *is* God, it is fitting that some Christians

---

[12] F I:175.

should dedicate their whole existence to seeking Him, to living in His presence, to offering Him their constant homage of adoration, thanksgiving, and petition. When a hermit asks for pardon and for favor, he thinks first of himself, realizing that he is a sinner—*sibi soli et Deo vacat*. But at the same time in his person he confesses the vileness of all humanity, so that all sinful humanity profits by his humility and by the favor which it draws down.[13]

The hermit serves his neighbors by prayer, of course, but not necessarily by praying for their intentions. Prayer contains a value in itself, independently of its object or occasion. Its effectiveness derives from the fact that it is addressed to God. It has been said that "it matters not that we know *for what* we pray, but rather *to Whom* we pray."[14] To formulate particular intentions may be a psychological device to sustain fervor; but this fervor springs from a realization that the Lord is almighty and worthy of our adoration, that He is Love and wishes to be loved.[15] To direct our prayer towards special objects which, however numerous, are always limited, is to reduce its universal range. God is the common Father of all men; by praying to Him, we necessarily help all men.

---

[13] Cf., chap. 16, pp. 0154-0159.

[14] Louis Bouyer, *The Meaning of the Monastic Life.* (New York: P. J. Kenedy & Sons, 1955.)

[15] Cf., supra chap. 10.

PART TWO

The Hermit Life

————————————

V.

FORMS OF THE HERMIT LIFE

The term *eremitic life* designates all the ways of living in solitude. We must now define it more closely by describing how it is carried on, particularly in the Camaldolese Order.

"For the many kinds of hermits may be divided into three groups. The first consists of men who, without vows of poverty, chastity, and obedience, without a rule, or profession, or a superior, live in solitary places wearing a religious garb. St. Benedict says that these are the worst brood of monks. They are censured in Church law and can be called "acephalous (headless) monsters." The second kind of hermits are those who, after a period of probation in cenobitic life, after pronouncing the three principal vows and being professed under an approved rule, leave the monastery and withdraw to live alone in solitude following the example of the

Fathers of Egypt. Such a life, as St. Jerome affirms, is more perfect than the cenobitic, but also much more perilous. It permits no companionship but requires that each be self-sufficient. Therefore it is no longer permitted in our day, as Holy Church now orders us to hear Mass often, to make our Confession, and to receive Communion: none of which can be done alone.

"There remains the third kind of hermit life: ours. It combines cenobitic and eremitic life. We make the vows of poverty, chastity, and obedience; we follow the Rule of St. Benedict oftentimes approved; we live under a superior, as a community united in constant obedience. Our discipline is in every way more austere than that of the cenobitic life. This hermit life, because it comprises the vows, the profession and the rule is not blameworthy as is the first kind of religious solitude. Because it gathers together a group of hermits for the same purpose, it is neither dangerous nor illicit like the second kind."[1]

Giustiniani describes in some detail this Camaldolese eremitic life. "The third form of eremitic life is that of men who withdraw either from the world, or from a monastery, and move away from all cities. They cut themselves off, as far as possible, from all association with men who live otherwise than they. They go to places absolutely isolated and remote:

---

[1] Q I:211.

to the top of mountains that are steep and difficult to climb, or to the bottom of deep and almost inaccessible valleys, to grottos unknown to other men, to the depths of well-hidden caves, to dense forests. Each lives there in a separate cell, but subject to a rule and to a superior, and bound by the three vows. Though they are in solitude, they are not absolutely alone, nor deprived of the help of their brothers. Even in the desert they are at home as in the Lord's mansion, and each profits by the society of all. For if one falls, the other lifts him up; if one is defeated by an enemy, that enemy is overpowered by many others; they all stimulate each other by their good works. They can provide for each other all the services which Holy Church prescribes as necessary to salvation. They escape entirely all the hindrances which endangered the salvation of the second kind of hermits. Their way of life is prudent: they enjoy the advantages of a life of submission and a life in society, but are released from the diverse tasks of monasteries; they relish the sweet and happy tranquility of solitude, but they escape the dangers of solitary life.

"This third kind of eremitic life owes its origin, by the inspiration of the Holy Spirit, to St. Romuald, patriarch of all the hermits of the West. In his day the Charterhouse had not yet been founded by St. Bruno, nor Vallombrosa by St. John Gualbert, nor Citeaux by St. Robert, nor Clairvaux by St. Bernard. And of course it was long before St. Francis and St. Dominic founded the Orders of Friars Minor and Preachers which now enlist an almost countless multitude of men and women. At that time the Western Church seemed no longer to have any religious life. Only a small number of abbots observed the Rule of St. Benedict, but so few were the monks under them, so neglected was proper monastic discipline, that they occupied rather than governed their monasteries. Then, like a light breaking through the clouds, appeared St. Romuald. He was the first to restore cenobitic life itself, for through him or after him the Lord stirred up the zeal of all others who undertook the reform of monasteries. Then in the desert of Camaldoli he introduced our form of eremitic life, exempt from the multiple activities found in monasteries, free of the harmful distractions occasioned by business matters and by association with laymen. It is both a pure cenobitic life (that is, purified from all hindrances) and a total eremitic life. It preserves all the advantages and precludes the disadvantages of both ways of life."[2]

In such an existence certain points of St. Benedict's Rule cannot be practised: some points of detail or observances are rendered impossible by the fact of living alone (such as the common dormitory), while certain prescriptions are not sufficiently severe for the hermit life, such as the regulations

---

[2] RVE f.40-41ʳ.

on food and drink.[3] But all the essentials of Benedictine life are safeguarded. We may say that the
Camaldolese hermit life is closer to community life
than the absolute solitude.[4] Thus the question of
determining if one can become a hermit immediately or of deciding the conditions necessary for a
change from cenobitic to eremitic life—such ques-
tions need not be asked, since the hermitage itself
is cenobitic.[5]

Are there, then, no degrees of progress within the
Camaldolese life? Does it offer no prospects of in-
creasing in perfection? This need is fulfilled by an
institution that is peculiar to it and is of the greatest
importance: *Reclusion*. Some of the monks are
allowed to withdraw from the others and to confine themselves in a cell from which they never
again emerge, in order that they may contemplate
heavenly truths in greater peace. They must first
have undergone a long period of testing and have
attained the mature age of forty or forty-five years.
Then, if after serious consideration they request it
insistently, the permission is granted. Always in our
midst there are some such recluses, good fathers
who stir up the fervor of the younger monks. In

---

[3] Q I:106.

[4] F + :145. A long text develops this idea, proves it by
examples, lists the advantages assured and the disadvantages avoided by the hermit life of Camaldoli.

[5] Giustiniani deals with this question, but from a more
speculative viewpoint and in relation to precedents of past
times in Q IV:312.

such reclusion their life is noticeably stricter as to fasting, psalmody, silence and other observances. However they are not at liberty to follow their own judgment, ideas, or desires without the express authorization of the superior. These segregated or secluded hermits—*inclusi*—are served by all the other hermits, who are called unsecluded—*aperti*— to distinguish them from the first. The superior provides for all their necessities, so that they need not concern themselves with anything earthly.[6] Reclusion indeed is Camaldolese hermit life in its ultimate perfection. "It belongs to those who crave more freedom for contemplation, and it is provided by God rather than by men. He who feels this craving ceases to associate with other men or even to see them: he cuts himself off from contact even with his fellow hermits. He is exempt from all human affairs. But he is not released from either the rule or the superior, nor is he deprived of help from others or of the Sacraments of the Church which cannot be supplied by himself. A little cell with a garden is assigned to him, either for a definite pre-arranged time or even, if he so desires, for always. There he is locked up, free of all care; there he can give his whole attention to God—*soli Deo vacare*."[7]

"The purpose of the hermits is to live with Christ —*cum Christo vivere*. Though the whole organism of the hermitage of Camaldoli aims at this goal, and

---

[6] F + :145.   [7] RVE f. 40ᵛ-41.

because it aims at it, St. Romuald, inspired by the Holy Ghost, presented a still more perfect way of life, combining the advantages of the two ways, cenobitic and eremitic, making possible a fuller realization of both ideals, in more complete security from the perils often encountered. In the happy days of past centuries this way of life had been adopted by a host of cenobites, hermits, and anchorites in the deserts of Egypt and in other regions of the East. But it was almost unknown amongst us. However, just as all regions and all seasons of the year are not embellished by the same fruits, so the divine Spirit does not confer the same gifts on each century. Religious who longed for the blessings of solitude either had to miss the benefits of obedience, attend to their daily needs and other necessities by themselves, and draw up their own individual rule of life—or else they had to renounce the tranquillity of solitude in order to preserve the treasures of obedience and poverty. Inspired by the Holy Ghost, St. Romuald gave the West this admirable institution of reclusion. Ever since that time there have always been Camoldolese hermits who, after leading the common life in the hermitage—*communis vita in eremo*—ardently sought freer contemplation and more perfect peace of soul, ardently longed to give their continual attention to God alone. With the consent of the superior and of their co-hermits, they have been locked into a cell with a garden where they continue as always to bear the yoke of the rule and where they strive to converse more intimately with God in heaven. It would be hard to imagine any happier life for those who are filled with zeal for prayer and for divine contemplation."[8]

Reclusion, thus, is not only a means whereby certain hermits carry out their personal vocation, but it is also a masterpiece of the hermit organization as such. It offers an example and inspires emulation, keeping within the hermitage the ideal of a more perfect life. Just as cenobitic life should keep its windows open on the vista of hermit life, so the eremitic life in its "unsecluded" form should retain possibilities of a more strict form. Without reclusion, the rule of the hermitage seems a maximum that cannot be surpassed; the hermit life is closed upon itself; rejecting all possibility of progress, it risks regress. By reclusion we are reminded that the hermitage is only a minimum; it can be surpassed by an existence even more remote from other men, by a seclusion that has its only outlook on heaven itself.

---

[8] RVE f. 130ᵛ-131.

VI.

THE REQUIREMENTS
OF THE HERMIT LIFE

To remain in solitude is the first condition of the hermit life. But to fulfill this condition truly, one must first be convinced of its importance: practice will result from conviction. Solitude has but one aim: to allow Christ to live in us. Because the Lord dwells in us, our hearts must not make room for Christ's enemies. Solitude is the fortified wall surrounding us to prevent their entry.[1] Solitude sets us free and once we are free we can realize the true worth of all things.

"By staying ever in my cell I am enabled to see a shadow, a remote but clear image of a life which is true life. Then do I scorn the life which is death rather than life, for this earthly life I value only as it helps me to acquire the one true life. I could never

---

[1] F I:155.

realize that—and I think that noone finds it easy—while I was surrounded physically and mentally by busy throngs, distracted by conversations, immersed in the swirling thoughts which in one way or another enter men's hearts."[2]

To understand how important solitude is for us, it is enough to recall its role in the history of our salvation. Let us hear its voice: "I am that solitary life which makes earthly men heavenly and carnal men spiritual. I gathered together the dispersed children of Israel, the men for whom the Son of God, sublime above all the heights of heaven, and exempt of all sin, willed to come down to the secret and hidden dwelling of the Virgin's womb. I shut the door on the secret oratory of that holy recluse, the solitary Mary, when the angel came to greet her. I am the solitary life that forms all things and by which all things receive that life without which there is no life. I am that solitude that often withdrew the true Life which was made flesh from the crowds. With me He spent nights in prayer, multiplied bread in the desert, overcame the devil in the desert, fasted, lived alone among the wild animals, and yet at the same time enjoyed the presence of the angels who served Him when He had no human company. When He wanted to show the glory of His transfiguration He left all others and led three Apostles alone with Him to the mountain. After-

[2] F I:47.

wards they, raising their eyes, saw noone, but only Jesus alone, for contemplation sees nothing but Him. Again Jesus entered solitude, separated even from His best-loved Apostles, to pray at length to His Father three times in His agony. He sweat blood and was comforted by an angel from heaven, not because He needed help but because He wanted to teach us that those who pray alone for a long time may hope for the comfort of an angel, even though the angel may not appear visibly.

"What can we say of that blessed first man, Adam, who was safe as long as he was alone, before his wife, his helpmate, sent him out into miserable exile. He had been put into that solitude of the terrestrial paradise in order that evil should not pervert his heart. . . . Abraham also was seated alone beneath the oak of Mambre when he saw three men and adored one. . . . He was alone when he received the promise of the Savior. . . . When John the Baptist was a child, who gave him a sweet and vast wilderness? Who instructed him in the desert? Who revealed to him the mystery of baptism? I, of course, I was with him in all things. Neither parents nor nurse helped him; wine did not warm him; soft and lovely garments did not clothe him. I alone was with him in all. I was adequate to all his needs."[3]

These benefits of solitude continue among us. "O blessed solitude which teaches humans to come to

---

[3] Q III:208.

their senses and to desire to see, as much as men can, the divine Majesty. O solitude, the foretaste of heaven's delight, the sample of celestial joy, granted to men living in the flesh! When holy souls weep in exile, impatient for the eternal joy that they hope to attain in the homeland, you alone, beloved solitude, relieve their long wait by glimpses of the bliss to come. O solitude, too little known by those who have not lived in your company! O solitude, never sufficiently praised: you change human misery to angelic happiness. If I understand rightly, you make angels of men. Though their bodies are detained here in this valley of woe, their spirits dwell in heaven. You enable the soul to adhere always to God the Creator, all good and almighty, who caresses the soul like a cherished bride. You delight it with divine words, as sweet as the kisses of a bridegroom. You proclaim the coming of the Holy Spirit—you not only *proclaim* Him, but you lead Him into the human heart as the dawn announces the day and also brings it to our eyes in the brightness of the sun. . . . Truly until I was alone, I never really lived. Until I was alone, I was not with myself. Until I was alone, I never drew near to my Creator."[4]

But how can such an exalted ideal be realized? The hermitage makes it practical. "For solitary places have always greatly helped true solitude of

_____

[4] F VII:101.

the soul. . . . St. Romuald chose the desert of Camaldoli because it was remote from all towns and
human dwellings, because the vast area of forests
around it hid it completely and made it almost inaccessible. Since then, settlements have appeared in
the district. If, therefore, the hermits truly wish to
safeguard their solitude, they should exert all their
efforts on the task of seeing that the forests around
the hermitage belonging to them, should not be
thinned out, but should be kept intact and developed. Permission to cut down pine trees for the
needs of the hermitage should never be granted
except with the express consent of the whole
Chapter. We should take care that the saplings are
not injured by either men or animals. The grove
enclosing the hermitage should be inviolable. Each
years four or five thousand pine saplings should be
planted to replace those that have withered or that
have had to be cut down. We should strive in every
way to avoid contact with laymen, even under the
pretext of offering alms or hospitality: this is not
through lack of kindness, but as a safeguard of solitude. In the hermitage no craft requiring the help
of laymen will be carried on. We must remove all
animals except those that are needed; these should
not be allowed to graze either by day or by night
within the hermitage grounds, nor should they remain there for long. Noone, of whatever rank, will
be authorized to enter the hermitage on horseback;
armor must be left at the gate, for the hermitage is

sacred: it is not fitting that men enter the Lord's house armed, nor should they trouble the peace of its inhabitants by speaking in loud voices.[5] All the territory within the grove of trees surrounding the cells, as well as the paths leading from the cells to the church, will be considered a cloister.[6] And hidden in each separate cell, the hermit may taste the utter peace of holy solitude."[7]

But he must not forget that "no physical solitude can confer peace of mind, without the help of the true solitude which is interior. . . . Perfection is not attained by details of place or time. The Lord has condemned those who believe that the Sabbath sanctifies man because the Sabbath itself is holy: it is man who sanctifies the Sabbath. Similarly, places do not sanctify men, but rather it is they who sanctify places."[8]

There is, then, no solitude without recollection and silence. Silence is the "principal adornment of solitude."[9] It must not be confused with mere absence of speech and noise, for it must be full of the divine presence. "The solitary enclosed in a narrow cell cuts himself off from human conversations only to speak with the Creator in prayer, or with himself in meditation. Otherwise, man who alone of all

---

[5] RVE f. 44^v-47; F A:19-21^v.

[6] RVE f. 97.   [7] RVE f. 41^v.   [8] Q I:37^v.

[9] Constitution of 1524, ed. P. Lugano, *La Congregazione camaldolese degli eremiti di Montecorona* (Frascati, 1908), p. 161.

animals has received the gifts of intelligence and speech, becomes a mute animal and perverts the holiness of silence. The silence of religious solitary life was not instituted to make us dumb animals, but to enable us to cease external conversation and to speak constantly to God in prayer or to speak usefully to ourselves in meditation. That is the meaning of religious silence: never to cease praying and meditating. The solitary may also write, either to sustain his own attention or to help his memory or to exhort his neighbour."[10]

If, then, the silence is filled with the thought of God, it becomes "a sweet and precious food. . . . Sweet, solitary stillness, wiser than Plato or Aristotle or all the other authors I used to read, lifts my soul closer to God, renders more translucent the veil through which I glimpse the Redeemer's infinite sublimity. I find that silence teaches me more than many conversation. Never did I perceive as clearly as now, the Lord's benefits. How grateful we should be to God who created us from nothing, created us in His image, created us with intelligence and will capable of turning to Him, created us nobler than all other creatures, all of which He made for us. Never did I realize all this as keenly in the world as I do in this solitude and the stillness."[11]

In practice eremitic silence comprises two de-

---

[10] Q III:79.   [11] F I:47.

grees. All conversation with laymen will be avoided, but among themselves the hermits will not be so severely bound to silence. Silence is the condition of true solitude. Like the remote location, it is a way to remove whatever disturbs peace of mind. Without silence, there is no solitude. One could withdraw to the most remote corners and be unknown to all men: but without silence there will never be anything but a mask of solitude.[12] We should not talk about or care to hear of wars and other happenings in the world, especially matters of state.[13] "To hear news of the world and of the town is a greater hindrance to spiritual progress than we think. So true is this that St. Benedict, who originated so many religious congregations, strictly enjoined those who go out on monastery business not to report on their return what they have seen or heard.[14] To retire from the world is of little use if the noise of the world invades the hermitage.

The hermits are allowed to have spiritual conversations among themselves. At certain times the superior will break the silence, so that the brothers may speak of necessary matters. There are recreation periods when they may walk about together on the outskirts of the hermitage. The days and the hours for all this are indicated in the Constitutions.[15]

It is even permitted to speak to the recluses.

---

[12] F A:22ᵛ. [13] RVE f. 42ᵛ. [14] F + :145.
[15] RVE f. 97-97ᵛ, 104-105, 107.

"During the festive week before Lent, on the days and at the hours when silence is broken, this is granted to whichever hermits wish it, only once for each. Each separately may approach each recluse and without entering his cell, speak with him through the window, moderately and briefly, unless a recluse should spontaneously refuse such visits because of his preference for silence and tranquillity."[16] So we see that silence is not absolute for anyone.

Besides "temperance in speech"[17] another guarantee of interior solitude is stability. It too is primarily a state of mind. "A change of place is sure to disturb the mind and cause many distractions. For a man does not move from place to place unless his mind changes from one purpose to another. The mind first begins to feel a slight change of this kind, which little by little induces the hermit to move to another place. Then the change of place, far from relieving the mind's inclination to change, only increases it. This need of change, at first so vague as to be barely conscious, becomes so strong once a man consents to it by physical change of place that it disturbs his whole life and even becomes evident to others. Thus we may deceive ourselves and mask our real intention if we first decide to change only our place but not our purpose. But the change of place readily induces us, and this time very

---

[16] RVE f. 98.   [17] F A:22.

definitely, to change our way of life. We must, therefore, avoid any change from the more perfect to the less perfect, or even the equally perfect, in fact, any change that is not very clearly in the direction of greater perfection. The monk who changes place, like the farmer who often transplants his trees, is cheated by his enemy of the fruits of his efforts. For a tree transplanted to a new field, even if the second spot be as good as or better than the first, may easily wither up and die unless it thrusts down its roots. In any case it bears fruit that is inferior and sour. So also with the monk whose roots have already reached deep into the ground. If the enemy persuade him to move to ground which he thinks better, he languishes miserably there or, seeking frequent changes and troubled by worldly matters, he becomes worse than laymen. If indeed the desire of heavenly truth still clings to his heart, the fruits of perfection that he produces are no longer as sweet or abundant as before the change. Wine, however good it may be, loses its taste and becomes sour if it is often transferred from one container to another, even if both containers are flawless. Material things are not marked merely by being moved: but our souls deteriorate, as they are like hot wax that retains the slightest imprint."[18]

One of the motives which suggests a change of place is the imperfection of the place where one

_____

[18] F I:155.

lives. But to seek to avoid every imperfection is a temptation. "Wherever there are men, there are imperfections which must be borne. In absolutely every community, however small it may be, each member has much to endure from the others, while they have to endure even more from him. Whenever men are together, even if it be only two of them, there are many causes of mutual hurt. He who refuses the virtue of mutual forbearance, so necessary to all human society, dissolves all social life. He becomes worse than the wildest savage, for men would derive no benefit from gathering together unless they managed to bear with each other to a certain extent. We must be convinced that every man is subject to some imperfection, but the man whose imperfection is most harmful of all is the one who resents others' imperfections and is unable to bear with them serenely. After all he too is imperfect, at least in that respect, whatever other great virtues he may have. What could be farther removed from God's goodness than to fail to bear, imperfect as we are, with the imperfections of our brothers, when the infinitely perfect Lord patiently tolerates the vices and outrages of so many thousands of souls. A monk who considered himself more perfect than his brethren was pained by their imperfections. He travelled to the desert with but one disciple. But he could not long bear the imperfection of even this one companion and he decided, therefore, to live entirely alone and thus avoid all imperfection. But as soon as he was alone he stumbled against a jug and broke it with a gesture of anger. Immediately he understood that the imperfection that needed correction was not in the habits of others, but in his own heart. . . . I recall having read long ago in pagan authors treating of the duties of husbands that a man should either tolerate or correct the faults of his wife: if he corrects them, he improves his wife; if he supports them, he himself becomes better. And it is always preferable to bear with others than to make others bear with us."[19]

The hermit will rarely have occasion to go out. "When we are here, we can say: *haec requies mea in saeculum saeculi, hic habitabo quoniam elegi eam.*[20] By tranquillity of the body, we can acquire tranquillity of mind. The monks who live in cities often go out of the monastery enclosure to enter the tumult of cities. And seeing certain things, or hearing certain rumors, they return, I fear, weaker and often more worried than when they left, bringing back with them some worldly care which will long trouble their minds. The solitary monk does not have this danger to face. If we leave our little cells, it is to enter a vast forest of high fir trees. The forest breeze and shade, the variegated flowers adorning the ground, the springs and brooks that rise and flow everywhere, the sweet warbling of

---

[19] Q IV:257.   [20] Ps. 131:14.

countless birds; Nothing in all that can disturb a tranquil soul. He who is downcast recovers his joy. All these creatures invite us to pray, to praise the Creator of all things. Then we return to our cells serenely happy."[21]

When a journey proves inevitable, we must learn to remain hermits even when travelling. "Hermits are not forbidden to mount horseback, any more than cenobites. But if anyone prefer to go on foot, either to practise humility or to mortify his body, he should not be obliged to take a horse, unless delay is harmful to the business at hand. On the contrary, all who are not impeded by age or weakness should make an effort to go on foot if the journey required of them take only one day. Those who profess the eremitic life should always accept what is hardest and most perfect. In the case of two hermits travelling together, particularly for a rather long distance, it is expressly forbidden that one go on horseback and the other on foot, even if one be a priest and the other a laybrother. They should both go on foot or both on horseback, unless they are forced to do otherwise because of the sickness of one of them or because of the lack of horses. Brothers should be equal in all things.

If a monk, as soon as he has passed the bounds of the hermitage, hastens to cast off the severe life he led there, it is a bad sign and reveals paltry observ-

---

[21] F + :145.

ance. Such a hermit shows that in following the
severe rule he was not so much inspired by love of
the rule, as forced by the necessities of the place.
To avoid this, hermits who for any reason leave the
hermitage should, as far as conditions allow, preserve the customs of eremitic life. Where that is
impossible, they should at least observe the Rule of
St. Benedict as it applies to cenobitic life. . . . They
should flee, as from a conflagration, from any monastery of nuns, of whatever order they be, even
Camaldolese.[22]. . . They should carry a little Bible.
. . . Unless they have to cross vast tracts of unin-
habited land, they should never consent to take food
for more than one day: if more is offered to them,
they should give the surplus to the poor. . . . Their
whole conduct should be marked by simplicity
rather than wariness. . . . They will not associate
with the nobles or eat at their tables. . . . They will
avoid long conversations with their hosts or companions and will strive to speak serenely of God,
not through vain glory, but for the benefit of their
neighbors. Above all they must ever praise God and
bless Him and ask His help for their benefactors.
They should not become too familiar with anyone:
Solus esse, solus iubilare, gaudere."[23]

Those who do not love solitude ("*solitudinis
amatores*"[24]) have no right to the title of hermits.
There must be a kind of devotion to the hermitage

---

[22] RVE f. 106, 106ᵛ.   [23] F + :217ᵛ.   [24] F A:19.

in order to justify the traditional title of *eremi cultores*.[25] In order to love solitude one must stay there. "The hermits should be glad to dwell in the hermitage through love of solitude which is so lovable and pleasing to holy souls."[26] Little by little solitude reveals its full delights to them. "They should learn to stay alone and to abstain from human conversations, to speak only of God. Then they will begin to taste the sweet serenity of solitary life and once they have absorbed this, they will find no difficulty but rather great joy in persevering there until death."[27] "They must strive to maintain constant stability in the hermitage and in the cell, in order that by God's grace their unremitting faithfulness will make it a pleasure to stay there. If they acquire the habit of leaving it, their cell will soon become a prison: he who often leaves it, spontaneously and without good reason, soon forgets it and then detests it. But he who rarely leaves it, and then for but a short time and by order of the superior, returns ever more gladly and finds it ever more delightful."[28]

To observe stability, it is not enough merely to

---

[25] This title is used, for instance, in the Chronicle of St. St. Benignus, P. L. 162,825. It is applied to St. John the Baptist in the hymn of First Vespers for his feast on June 24th in the Roman Breviary. The same title is found inscribed at the gate of the Camaldolese Sacred Hermitage of Frascati.

[26] F A:21.   [27] F A:22ᶜ.   [28] RVE f. 102, 102ᵛ.

refrain from going out. Even within the cell insta-
bility must be avoided. "Hermits should so ruthlessly uproot the vice of rambling about that even
even within the cell they should prefer to stay
invariably in the same spot at the same occupation.
Those who have less taste for stability might be
seized by restlessness or spurred by some devil or
other, so that they would spend the whole day
wandering from one room to another of their
hermitage, taking up several tasks at once only to
drop them as quickly. On the contrary, they should
strive to be ever in the same place at the same task,
not yielding easily to boredom or the need for
change. Our fathers in the eremitic life have always
declared this: for the fretful, restless hermit, the
cell is a prison and a torture chamber, a source of
great anguish. But for the hermit who is calm and
mindful of stability, the cell and the silence offer a
safe refuge against all temptations, a place of re-
freshment, a beginning of paradise."[29]

---

[29] RVE f. 102ᵛ.

VII.

THE OCCUPATIONS OF
THE HERMIT LIFE

The hermit in his solitude is exempt from all the ordinary occupations of other men. In this sense the solitary life is a life of leisure. Contrary to appearances, however, it is a very busy leisure, a leisure full of work: *negotiosissimum otium*.[1] It must be so: otherwise eremitic life would be worthless rather than useful. The Rule, therefore, formally emphasizes the obligation to fill every hour with definite tasks.

"All must keep busy at manual work during the proper and prescribed time for it. Then they must devote other definite hours to reading, prayer, and other spiritual exercises, so that the whole length of the day and night may seem short and insufficient. There should always be more to do than

---

[1] RVE f. 102ᵛ.

there is time for. Woe to him who begins to find his days dragging."[2]

How, in practice, should the use of time be organized? Giustiniani has left us two individual time tables, the first addressed to one of his hermits, the other written in the form of a soliloquy. They are characterized by perfect equilibrium of the body's and the spirit's needs. With winning naturalness the author passes from the most concrete details to wholly sublime considerations. We can see this in a few examples:

"When you go to bed, before falling asleep, read a book of history, preferably the life of a saint or some other easy and pleasant subject. Never cover more than one octavo page, because short and easy reading best suits that time of night. . . . Your confessions should be brief, simple, and without repetitions: just tell your sins without entering into details of when and how; do not seek or give advice; do not discuss any other matter; do not refer to past confessions. . . . Never fail to set the table for meals, for you should never eat in a negligent way. If you have no table or bowl, or if they are dirty, ask for clean ones and always eat in a dignified and gentlemanly way. . . . After Vespers spend the time until Compline at manual work in common, or if there is no community work, do then all the tasks that you can save for that time: washing your clothes, fetching wood or water, sweeping the cell or the Church, and so on. Get all these jobs done ahead of time for the next day. . . . Each time you return to the cell after the Office, genuflect and say a short prayer, at least a Pater or an Ave or else: *Domine Jesu, adoro te, miserere mei et adjuva me.* Keep your cell very clean and tidy and well swept (when I say "cell" I include also the garden and the fountain, etc. that are in front of it). Keep your body and your clothes clean; take every precaution against lice, which are a hindrance to the spiritual life. Be humble enough to ask the lay brothers to help you in such tasks as the laundry. But we should not *order* but rather humbly *request* others to do what we cannot do or do not know how to do for ourselves. Often it is as great an act of charity to be served as it is to serve. To avoid falling asleep at prayer keep erect, leaning little or not at all."[3]

You should always keep a balance in favor of spiritual activity.

"Do manual work to the extent that it serves practical needs, keeps you healthy, makes you humble, and provides necessary relaxation. Prefer simple menial tasks, those which help your brothers more than yourself. If there is no need for such work or if your health does not require it, then concentrate on spiritual, rather than physical exercises. Just as the soul is not made for the sake of the body, but

[3] Q III:187; Q III:52.

the body for the soul, so physical work should be subordinate to spiritual activity."[4]

But what are these spiritual occupations? They are innumerable and each is endless. The most enlightening explanation of how a contemplative soul keeps busy attending to "itself alone and God" is a long rhapsody which we quote in part:

"Those who have never experienced the occupations of religious leisure imagine that a solitary is constantly depressed by inactivity and idleness, very bored, full of regrets, like a man asleep or a brute beast that passes the time doing nothing. But, my Lord God, I, in my solitude, speak to You. How it delights me to speak to You and when I speak to You, I cannot lie. I declare that long years of experience have proved that the more I am solitary, the less I am idle. Only when I am not solitary am I inert, subject to boredom and regret. Never do the days seem so short, the nights so brief, the passage of time so rapid as when I can enjoy beloved solitude, free of all outside occupation and far from all company. It seems to me that in this, more than in any other way of life, occupations are both lacking and superabundant. No indeed, the life of solitaries is not what some may imagine, inactive and idle. More than any other life, it is active and busy. Is it idleness to read to study, to compose, to write? Is it idleness to examine our conscience, to regulate

---

[4] Q III:52.

our passions, to recall our past life, to put in order our present state, to provide wisely for the future? Is it idleness to repent our past sins, to combat temptation and inordinate desires, to arm ourselves in advance against the proximate occasions of sin and worry, to think of death and to picture it vividly so that it may not catch us unawares? Is it idleness to meditate on human and divine truths which alone enthrall noble minds, to ponder these truths, not in haphazard daydreams, but with order and concentration? Is it idleness to raise our voices frequently by day and by night in psalms, canticles, and hymns, praising God, and thanking Him for all His benefits? Or to praise Him still more eloquently and truly by mental prayer that raises us as high as mortal man can come to the divine Majesty? Thus may we, as it were, transcend, insofar as man is able, this world and converse in heaven with the blessed spirits, the holy Angels and the One who created them and us. Thus may we in some way gaze on the ineffable and indescribable perfections of God reflected by analogy as in a mirror. Is it idleness to inspire and exhort others to such a life by speaking to those present and by writing to those absent? Is it idleness to wear cheap, rough garments, to eat poorly and meagerly, to keep long vigils, to do menial and strenuous work? By these means we can tame the pride of life, curb the desires of the flesh, train the body ever to serve and obey the soul and reason. Do you maintain that all these activities and many other similar practices of hermits are more inertia, boredom, lethargy? Instead you must admit that the solitary life is more active and busy than any other, busy not at external corporal tasks or worldly business, but full of nobler and more fruitful activities, such interior and spiritual tasks as best suit the part of man that is immortal.

"How is it with other solitaries, I do not know. I can easily believe that each of them manages the leisure of his solitude better than I. But You know, Lord, and You can see that the more solitary I am, the more tasks occur that I ought to do and want to do. But unfortunately through lack of time I must put aside some projects, as if I wanted to save them for another day. Those that I do undertake are often left uncompleted because I lack time to finish them as I should or as best I could, with God's help. How often in the leisure of solitude I have postponed mental prayer because I was absorbed and delighted in reading! My attention to prayer, weak and cold as it is, keeps me from reading. How often the effort to write down a few ideas for my own sake or to help others has hindered me from giving due time to prayer and study! How often, because of one of these occupations, I have postponed the time for dinner or deprived my body, as now, of the hours of needed rest! I would like to do more; each task seems essential, each attracts me strongly. Yet I do none perfectly, or even as well as I might, with divine help, if I had enough time and if I thought of only one at a time.

"Whoever may believe and say that solitaries are inactive and idle, I shall never cease thinking and saying that no other life is as active and busy as that of God's servants, the hermits. For a time, longer than I would have liked, I experienced worldly affairs and the worries of governing a Congregation. In these matter I always seemed impeded more by lack of ability, application, and diligence than by lack of time. With the business of active life, the more I do, the less there is to do. But in matters of the solitary life, the more ability, application, and diligence I muster, the more I always find to do and the less time to do it. In solitary leisure, that is, the contemplative life, the more I do, the more I see to be done. In active life it is generally enough to plan and arrange matters well and then delegate the work to others. But the duties of contemplative life must all, with God's help, be arranged and performed by ourselves. The former can, for the most part, be arranged and carried on while eating or walking about. The latter are of such nature that each requires an entirely free mind and absorbs the whole self.

"To express what I mean I will give an example. To perform worldly duties, however many they may be, one soul suffices. But it seems to me that even a hundred souls would not suffice for the duties of the life of leisure. In any case I am sure that all the hundred could be occupied worthily and fruitfully. Men who are engaged in secular affairs, especially those in authority, need only one soul and they have plenty of time at their disposal. Sometimes they even feel the need of distraction and seek out pastimes to prevent boredom. They take up games and music and all sorts of absurdities characteristic of senseless and inane persons. A hermit finds that one soul alone is not enough for him to serve God as he would like and ought and perhaps could. He would like to have a hundred souls and if he had them, he is sure that he could keep them all busy: he even doubts if that many would be sufficient. He takes great care in regulating his time. He keeps vigil, eats only once a day, and avoids all extraneous occupation in order to make his days and nights longer than they are for other men. In spite of all this he has too little time and too much work. On the other hand, men who are occupied in base worldly activities, in sleep, in debauchery, in laughter, in improper conversations loathe as if it were death itself the idea of being alone and recollected, of reflecting on themselves. These are the very men, oddly enough, who accuse hermits of being idle, useless, and sterile, who consider them more gluttons. We must pardon such men and pity them, for they are mistaken. They stray from the way of truth by thus judging and condemning others while they themselves wander into still greater peril by their own conduct. Lord

God, deign to pardon them and by paths known only to Your Majesty, lead them to eternal light so that they may be liberated from the darkness of this world and may know this truth and many others that are still hidden from them.

But returning to myself: now that by your grace, Lord, I am more solitary than ever before, I know that I cannot find time to do all I should do and would like to do in Your service. . . . Oh, how many books I would like to read, were it not for lack of time and the demands of other duties! Not that I yearn to reread the books of pagan philosophers and poets, for I regret and repent having devoted more time than I should have to such study. But I would like to read many commentaries that would reveal the hidden and spiritual sense of your holy Scriptures. I would like to read many works that might spur my soul to piety and compunction, moral treatises that would help me to distinguish one kind of leprosy from another, one sin from another. Oh, how I wish I could carry your holy Gospels next to my heart, ever in my hand as did the holy Virgin St. Cecilia, that I might never interrupt day or night that divine study! You know, Lord, that I have often intended to do so; but either I lacked time or my soul was busy at other things. Not only would I like to read, but I need to strive earnestly to understand what is read, to concentrate on the meaning rather then the words, to compare the opinions of various theologians, or various passages of one of them, to follow also the other practices of serious scholars. . . .

"To read and to write are truly the easiest tasks, the least absorbing and the least perfect of the solitary's life. . . . We must also meditate, pray, and rise as high as we can in the contemplation of heavenly truths. We must feel bitter repentance of the ill-used days of our life; we must examine, describe, control, regulate, moderate the passions of the present time; we must pledge our future to God's service; we must think of death and prepare for it. After such meditation on visible and created reality, what can we say of the quest of the invisible reality of God? What can we say of mental prayer? We must thank you, Lord, for your favors, thank you for having created us and for having provided the whole visible world for our use. We must praise you and thank you for the blessing of the Redemption that you accomplished, you who become incarnate, who lived among men, who taught them by example and by preaching, who died and was raised to life for them. We must thank you for the countless marvellous blessings that you have granted to all humanity, for the particular blessings that you gave us and that you continue to bestow each day. We must praise you, adore you, offer you the homage of latria or adoration that is due to you alone. Our intellects and our wills must unite to invoke you, to offer and consecrate ourselves to your service, to submit and conform to your will, to desire you alone and your glory, to strive to know you ever better, to love you to yearn towards you, to cling to you, to be united to you, to be transformed in you, to disappear and be annihilated in you. How many complex aspects there are in the practice of meditation and in the contemplation of your invisible and ineffable perfections: your eternity, omnipotence, immensity, wisdom, ineffable charity, and the justice that is inseparable from your mercy. You, alone, Lord, are a fathomless abyss, immense, vast enough to absorb the attention of a countless multitude of souls, as you enthrall the countless multitudes of heavenly spirits.

"Men immersed in worldly affairs should not say that solitaries are inactive or idle. If by *idle* they mean that hermits neither buy nor sell nor build nor navigate nor engage in lawsuits nor raise children, then such a condemnation would likewise apply to the holy Angels of God who could be termed idle, inactive, and useless. With differences of manner and degree, the solitary undertakes the same activities as the Blessed Spirits. With the Seraphim he tirelessly loves the Creator; with the Cherubim he constantly thinks of God alone; with the Thrones he strives to make his own soul a temple of the Supreme Creator; and likewise for all the other angelic functions. In all things he tries to act like the angels. Moreover, since the hermit is a man he must attend to all sorts of corporal actions . . . which the angelic spirits never encounter.

So it is that a hermit could be considered even less idle than an angel, since the hermit devotes to God's service not only the operations of his soul but also his exterior actions. He lifts his voice to praise your divine Majesty by day and by night. He offers an example of humility, patience, and all the virtues. He celebrates the all-holy mysteries of the Mass, offering the salutary Sacrifice of the Sacred Body and Precious Blood of Jesus, as well as receiving that Body as his food often, almost daily. He prepares for this mystery, contemplating the divine mercy, offering thanks for such a heavenly gift, such an extraordinary boon. In addition, since the hermit, however holy he may be, still treads the slippery and dusty path of our human pilgrimage, he must admit how often his feet, that is, his affections, are sullied by the mud of some vain and harmful concupiscence or by the dust of human praise. He must then undertake the tedious task of purification. From this the angelic spirits are exempt, for they are free of such weakness. At every step, that is, in every act, the hermit must take tremendous precautions to avoid stepping into the mud or the dust. In spite of all this effort, so frail is human nature and so numerous are the perils of this life that he must frequently be cleansed and washed by contrition, penance, and confession. He must seek new strength in the firm purpose to watch over himself by greater care in the future. I need hardly mention, as it proves little or nothing, the hermit's tears, as he weeps through sorrow at having offended God or by excess of joy, as he welcomes heavenly favors and the divine presence within him. He weeps in his impatient longing for his heavenly home; he weeps in his burning desire to see You, oh Lord Jesus Christ, and to enjoy the beatific vision of Your presence. I shall not describe the spiritual conversations of the hermit with his Guardian angel, with the other blessed spirits, and with the souls of those whom he has loved in this world and whom he now loves more then ever since they left him, especially those whose virtue was so great that he may suppose them already happy in heaven.

"If, after such an enumeration of important activity, anyone can still maintain that hermits are idle, inactive, and subject to boredom, I confess that I am willing and even glad to be idle and inactive in that way than to be active in the manner of worldings. Of this I am not ashamed. Rather I am proud of being chosen to enter your service, Lord Jesus Christ, and to be disdained and condemned as inactive and useless. Being a religious and a hermit, I leave to others the worldly affairs in which they judge themselves to be so active, so worthily employed, so important. In exchange for their low opinion of us, I consider *them* to be like children who fashion little houses of straw and mud or play all day with pebbles as if with precious gems, so foolish that they are comical. When I see the worldlings engrossed and busy all day long with earthly matters, which are nothing but scattered straw; when I see them place such a high value on the treasures of this life, which are but mud and pebbles, then I cannot say that I laugh, but I feel a great pity. Knowing that this world passes away and contains nothing that endures, I have withdrawn from it as much as I can by leading a religious life in solitude. All my thoughts and desires become so many steps on the path to the true homeland in heaven. Weak as I am, I drive myself onward and spur others to the same destination. On this journey, which to me seem nowise idle or inactive but rather active and busy, I ever praise You, my Lord, and strive to know and love You always, until through Your mercy, I may reach that land where I can endlessly know You, perfectly love You, eternally praise You. There I may sleep and rest in peace with You, rest in the peace that is not idle and inactive but is busier than all other business, the peace which You enjoy, and with You all the Blessed Spirits. Amen."[5]

There have been several references to the angels in this text which lists the hermit's occupations. Because angels adore God constantly they offer the ideal of a life wholly consecrated to the divine praise. But the hermit must do more than adore. Unlike the angels, he belongs to this sinful world

---

[5] Q IV bis:92.

and he must do penance. Moreover, he still lives by faith, not by vision. In this double aspect he has other models: the prophets and the penitents. Elias was "the first to introduce eremitic life."[6] John the Baptist "fled from cities and from men."[7] Both these prophets awaited the revelation of the Lord. But perhaps an even better model than them, the supreme type of the eremitic life is Mary Magdalen, if we admit that the Gosepls refer to her in telling of the woman who wept for her sins and then lived in friendship with the Lord, she knelt before Him at the banquet in the home of Simon the Pharisee; she remained at the Lord's feet when He hung on the Cross; she again threw herself at His feet after His resurrection.[8]

"That Mary of Magdala is my longtime patron. I see her everywhere beside Jesus: on His journeys, at His meals, at the foot of the cross, at the tomb, at the resurrection."[9]

Her entire life, therefore, and her very constancy in following the Lord everywhere, provides a model for the hermit. "If you wish to lead the life of a solitary, imitate Mary Magdalen in all things.

---

[6] Q II:103. This theme is developed at length.

[7] Q I:192. [8] F VIII:30.

[9] Q I:130. The life and deeds of Mary Magdalen are treated here at great length. She is called "*quella incomparabile amatrice di Gesu,*" that incomparable lover of Jesus. At the end of the text (f. 158ᵛ-159ᵛ) Giustiniani tries to prove that the same person is referred to in all the incidents here ascribed to Mary Magdalen.

In her are found all the elements of the hermit life."
By what the Gospel tells of her and by what is
recorded of her subsequent life, Mary Magdalen
teaches the hermit all his duties. "Do more than kiss
the feet of Christ: remain at His feet. . . . Do not
abandon solitude for the sake of activity. . . . Withdraw from everything and everyone. Live with
Christ utterly alone, seeking no other solace, no
other love. Await the dissolution of the body, heeding naught but yourself and Christ, or rather, Christ
alone, and yourself in Christ."[10]

---

[10] F VII:140ᵛ; further development in Q II:134.

PART THREE

The Hermit's Prayer

VIII.

THE HERMIT'S ONLY TEACHER

The hermit's spiritual occupations are divided into three kinds which the rule clearly distinguishes:

"Whenever the hermits are not engaged in manual work, their whole time should be devoted to study, psalmody, and prayer."[1] Such is the total program: *study*, which really means careful attention given to the Holy Scripture; Psalms in its many uses; prayer, both public and private. These three activities complement each other and all aim at the same goal of union with God. All three are equally necessary.

Study is permitted only insofar as it forms a preparation for the other two activities. In this regard it plays a very important role and is, indeed, absolutely necessary to the hermit. Once the hermit

---

[1] RVE f. 84ᵛ.

understands *why* he studies, he will know also *how* to study. Giustiniani often repeats this important principle: "He who believes that Jesus Christ is true God and true man need not look elsewhere for moral discipline, for doctrine, nor for examples among philosophers and other admirable men. It is sufficient that he read and reread the holy Gospels which display to everyone the doctrine and example of Jesus Christ. He also believes that Jesus Christ is true God and true man need not seek to learn from any other master the meaning of virtue and of life, of good and of evil, of truth and of falsehood. He has in Christ the ineffable divine Wisdom teaching all we need to know of these matters. He need not look to any other great and famous men to enlighten him by the example of their lives. In Jesus Christ, true man as well as true God, he has at hand all the most brilliant examples of the highest virtues fused in Him more perfectly than in any man who is nothing more than a man, devoid of any flaw or defect. And so he should not seek any other teacher or master."[2]

Christ is the only master; Christ is the only book, "the book that contains all divine wisdom. My book should be Jesus Christ on the Cross: a book entirely written with His precious Blood that is the price of my soul and the redemption of the world. The five chapters of this book are the five sacred wounds.

---

[2] Q II:52.

I want to study that one book alone, and other books only as they comment on it. Did not St. Paul say that he no longer knew anything but Jesus Christ, Jesus Christ crucified? It is vanity to seek to know anything else at all. But this book must be read in silence."[3]

"Christians must be blind if, while believing in Jesus Christ, they imagine that they can learn the truth in any other school but His or from any other author but Christ and His holy Gospels."[4]

All other true doctrine derives from His, and in particular, all that the Fathers of the Church have written is inspired by Him and should lead to Him. "Christian writers have produced many and diverse writings: some have studied in detail one particular mystery of Christianity; others have developed other aspects, using different methods and displaying more or less subtility. They have also described the examples furnished by holy men of the times before Christ or since His coming. But we learn most and benefit most from the encounter with the mystery of Christ Himself, our Redeemer. For we are, indeed, called *Christians* on account of Christ, and Christ is the Son of God, the uncreated Word, the divine Truth who could not be mistaken in His teaching. On the other hand, He took on our human nature, though exempt from the flaws of original sin or of our actual sins. His doctrine, therefore, is

---

[3] F I:49.   [4] F I:47.

necessarily the holiest possible, more perfect than that of any other man who has ever lived, who lives now, or who will live in the future. No teaching can surpass that in which we behold Our Lord and Redeemer Jesus, in His roles as the light, the guide, the mirror, the infallible rule of life, the one true tutor. "We should always have recourse to original sources: but all that has been said or written throughout Christianity has its source in Him. . . . Jesus Christ is a book in which men who understand the language find a resumé of all doctrine, all discipline, all controversy, all learning, all exhortation which have expressed or ever will express divine truth from the beginning to the end of the world. The sacred writers have never conveyed more than a particle of the total doctrine contained in this book; they have been little streams in which flows the water of that inexhaustible fountain. Each of them writes only one chapter, one short paragraph of the blessed book that is Jesus Christ, the abyss and source of all intellectual and moral truth."[5]

This conviction determines how one should proceed to acquire knowledge in union with Jesus Christ. After stating the general principles, the Rule then provides detailed practical advice on the proper method of study. "The hermits are allowed to undertake any study that is not forbidden by the Church, providing that they avoid banned books

---

[5] Q III:172.

or superstitious books. Everything else may be read by each according to his capacity. Undoubtedly those who study holy Scripture rather than profane works have chosen the better part, for the latter are as nothing compared to the former. Those, therefore, who have made sufficient progress to find all their delight in the continual study of Holy Scripture without the help of any secular books, should abstain from reading anything else. But those who, either to improve their Latin or to acquire other useful knowledge, need to study other matters, may do so, but without forgetting that they should ever tend towards the ultimate goal of a better knowledge of Holy Scripture. Moreover during the days and hours when silence may be broken, two or more hermits together may discuss some point of their studies, give each other lessons or explain texts to each other, especially in books by Christian authors. . . . When religious who are in the habit of preaching visit the hermitage, the Superior will ask them to speak to the hermits as a means of encouragement. . . . All the hermits may, without any special permission, enter the library of the hermitage where the books must be arranged in good order. A catalogue of all the books will be kept and any hermit may have the Superior's permission to take to his cell whatever volumes he may need, provided he furnish the Library with written records of the books he has taken. . . . Each year new books should be bought, whichever seem the best and the most useful: no year should pass without at least ten gold crowns being spent on books. . . . All this is arranged because experience has proved that in religious souls study stimulates all the virtues."[6]

The Rule of 1524 goes a step further by providing a new office: "To encourage the brothers to study the General Chapter will each year designate one or more lectors chosen among the most competent hermits. Every day they should read and explain to the others a passage of Holy Scripture. The Superiors should also see to it that the hermits who are more studious and better able to learn should receive instruction from the lectors."[7]

Throughout his life Blessed Paul preached by his own example what he ordered regarding study. He never ceased his work of scholarship, especially in the domain of theology. True, he continued to write on philosophical subjects:[8] he drew up a list of the writings of Aristotle, Plato, and Plotinus, as well as a list of the names of Platonic and Peripatetic philosophers.[9] He took notes on the classical authors,[10] but more particularly on the Fathers of the Church: Origen, Rufinus, Eusebius of Caesarea,[11] St. Augustine, Cassian, St. Gregory the Great, Cassiodorus, the Pseudo-Dionysius, and St. Bernard. He read St. Thomas, St. Albertus Magnus,

---

[6] RVE f. 84ᵛ-85.   [7] Ed. Lugano, p. 156.   [8] F VII:201.
[9] F VII:168-169.   [10] F VII:170.   [11] Q I:3,15,16.

and Dante.[12] He translated into Italian certain short treatises attributed to St. Basil, to St. Bernard, and to Richard of St. Victor.[13] He did not neglect either Canon Law or Church History. He began a treatise on Interdictions[14] and he made a summary of Sozomenus' *Ecclesiastical History*.[15] He made notes on the history of monasticism[16] and of what he called "the Camaldolese republic."[16a] He made a list of all those who had written against the Koran since the time of Peter the Venerable.[17] In a treatise against superstition he alluded to history, to law, to the Fathers of the Church, and to St. Thomas.[18] But on the other hand, to be within reach of all men, he composed for the novices who were illiterate a summary of Christ's teaching as contained in the Gospels.[19]

Thus we see that he was a model of vast culture —vast, but not diffuse, for it was entirely focused on the Incarnate Son of God. Its primary source of growth is Holy Scripture and indeed his writings are mostly a commentary on Scripture as the Bible can solve all problems much better than any other book.[20] The Bible possesses a special power to glorify the divine Name and to attract men towards

---

[12] F II, Q I, F VII, *passim.*   [13] Q I:181, 187.
[14] F VII:19ᵛ.   [15] F VII:163-166ᵛ.   [16] F VII:198ᵛ.
[16a] F VII:110ᵛ.   [17] F + :220.   [18] F + :182.
[19] F VIII:22.
[20] Q II:19—with reference to Job and the problem of evil.

the knowledge and the love of God. To hear it read is always profitable, for it cannot fail to affect the souls of those listening. But of course they must understand it. Therefore it is desirable that good translations be made in every country and that these be read in the Churches in the language that the people understand."[21]

The source of all perfection in the Bible is the Gospel, for the reasons that we have already stated. As Christ is both God and man, His teaching possesses divine authority and is intended for every man. He offers both words and example together.[22] Never, then, showed we tire of reading the Gospels. "It is reported that Arcesilas loved Homer so much that he read him before falling asleep, resumed the book on awaking, and took care that nothing could prevent his reading it. But the supreme philosophy of Christ is contained in the Gospels. Let us, therefore, follow Arcesilas; let us read a few pages on the life and teaching of Christ each morning and again in the evening. Let us also find Christ in St. Paul. Let us love Christ and do what He loves. Did He not say: 'He who loves me keeps my Word'? Our memory should be filled with His Words. Those who fail to read the Gospels find it difficult to love Christ."[23]

The conclusion of the Rule is an invitation to

---

[21] F I:184. Giustiniani states that he intends to present such a plan to Pope Leo X.

[22] Q IV:166; cf. Q III:104ᵛ.   [23] F + :96.

have recourse constantly to the Gospels. "If a man aims at interior perfection in the eremitic religious life, he must first of all read the Gospels and the best commentaries on it, that is, the Epistles of the Holy Apostles, for they do no more than explain the Gospel teaching."[24] The Fathers of the Church should be read because they speak of Jesus and set forth His teaching. Blessed Giustiniani rejoiced to live in their company.[24a] He especially exalted the one whom he named "our Christian Sallust and our Christian Cicero, Pope St. Leo the Great."[25]

"I name him so because in all his writings this great Doctor teaches and proves but one thing: Jesus Christ is true God and true man. This is a truth that contains all the mysteries and all the sacraments of evangelical perfection."[26]

The authority of the Gospels is based on the Incarnation[27] and therefore, to read the Gospels focuses the mind on that great mystery by which "the Lord God became a recluse in the womb of the Virgin Mary."[28] The Incarnation is continued in the Holy Eucharist and this mystery also inspired Blessed Giustiniani with sublime utterances.[29]

But why does this hermit write so copiously? He

---

[24] RVE f. 140ᵛ.

[24a] F I:224; cf. *un humaniste ermite*, p. 56.

[25] Q II:51.

[26] *Ibid.* In F II:107 there are notes on St. Leo's writings about the Incarnation.

[27] RVE f. 141.   [28] F I:47.   [29] F II:100.

himself tells us: "I write less what I have learned than what I am trying to learn, for I am one of those who make progress by writing. I have often noticed that by writing I understood what I could not grasp by reading, meditating, or praying."[30] Thus he studies mainly for the sake of study and as an aid to contemplation, though the possibility of usefulness to others is not excluded. In the two timetables which he drew up, one for himself, the other for one of his hermits he provided for this activity: *utilis scriptio*—each day write something of use to yourself or to your neighbor; once you have begun writing something, finish it; do not drop it without good reason."[31] Elsewhere he advised: "Write something for the common good or for your own consolation."[32] Study is an obligation of the eremitic life. While the hermit's purpose is not to write for the benefit of others, yet that may become one of the fruits of his contemplation, the result and the expression of a culture that is entirely God-centered.

---

[30] Q III:104ᵛ.   [31] Q III:52.   [32] Q III:187.

IX.

THE DIVINE CHANT

Like study, psalmody, in the traditional sense of the term, also nourishes and expresses the hermit's spiritual life. By psalmody we mean both the celebration of the Divine Office, where the Psalms play such an important role, as well as the private recitation of the psalter.

Eremitic liturgy should be marked by the simplicity and austerity typical of solitary life. In Giustiniani this need is accentuated by his determination to react against the pomp so prevalent at the time of the Renaissance. These two motives affect every detail and the whole tenor of the Liturgy. "In the choir we remember that the monk's function is to weep for himself and for the world; we do not sing, except very rarely: we should not seek to please men."[1] "You must not take pleasure

---

[1] F + :145.

in the pomp of processions."[2] "A single bell will announce the time for the Divine Office. In cities the superfluous chiming of sets of several different bells may serve a good purpose by stirring up the people's piety and by summoning crowds: the cenobites, therefore, tolerate them. But they are quite contrary to eremitic serenity and purity."[3] . . ."In accord with *tradition*, the hermits never sing: they intone the Divine Office in plain chant with voices neither too low nor too high nor too loud, but devoutly, and yet with virile joy. The hermit's function is not to sing and exult, but to weep and to do penance."[4]

"The chant must be calm: neither too slow nor too quick. We should avoid haste and confusion in order to pronounce the words distinctly and clearly. One choir must never begin before the other has finished. Make the pause in the middle of each verse. . . . On solemn feasts the chant should be slower and more clear, and also the night Office during Winter, taking advantage of the longer nights."[5]

Countless details deal with psalmody which by itself is the subject of more regulations than all the rest of the Office, being indeed its most important part. The complete Psalter must be kept in mind in drawing up the calendar or in classifying feasts.

---

[2] RVE f. 42.   [3] RVE f. 61.
[4] RVE f. 67ᵛ.   [5] RVE f. 68ʳ.

"We must reduce the number of saints' feasts to prevent the monotony of saying the same psalms all year long. Two principles must govern the assignment of Scriptural texts in the liturgy: the whole Bible should be read each year and the whole Psalter should be recited in common each week."[6]

In addition to the liturgical Psalms, one of the traditional eremitic practices is "to rejoice each day in the private recitation of Psalms."[7] These Psalms are also minutely regulated. The number of Psalms to recite varies according to the seasons and according to the time available after the recitation of the Divine Office. More time is given to this during certain periods, such as Lent. Also a greater number are said by the recluses than by the other hermits. But some time must always be provided for this purpose.[8] It must not, however, become a tedious burden. The Rule of 1524 reduced the assignment to fifty Psalms a day in order to allow more time for meditation. Moreover, of these fifty psalms, half could be replaced by reading. "And it is understood that these Psalms may be said by enunciating the words or by reciting them mentally.[9] What is essential is never to lose sight of the purpose of these rules: "Recite these Psalms in a way that will bring some fruit of piety or of spiritual understanding."[10]

Blessed Giustiniani often expressed praise of what

---

[6] RVE f. 70ʳ-71ᵛ. [7] RVE f. 42ᵛ. [8] RVE f. 81-82.
[9] Ed. Lugano, p. 157. [10] Q III:52.

he called "the divine canticles,"[11] which so far surpass all the learning of philosophers.[12] But he in-
sisted that they be studied to be appreciated. He
himself studied them intensively. He translated and
explained from the Greek certain verses that had a
somewhat different meaning in the Vulgate.[13] To
attain a deeper insight into the meaning of the
Psalms, he wished he could have learned Hebrew
and he consulted those who did know it. "I greatly
desire a commentary on Psalm 144 which in
Hebrew is alphabetic. Study it in the Hebrew so
that you can enlighten me. I seem to recall that
Pico de la Mirandola explained it, but I do not have
his books here."[14] Giustiniani recommended that
emphasis should be primarily on the literal sense.
"In reciting the Psalms, I would like you, if possible,
to rein in your spirited intellect and turn aside for
a while from all mystical or allegorical senses to
consider purely and simply the literal meaning, that
is, what our friend David meant at the moment he
composed the Psalms. Then you will see how incomparably greater Scripture is than any poet or
philosopher. David is truly a great philosopher, as
he contemplates in his Psalms God's lofty mysteries,
the creatures of His making, and the qualities of
our souls."[15]. . ."Now that you have a tutor to teach
you Hebrew, have him read you the Psalms, the

---

[11] Q IV *bis* 229.   [12] F II:122ᵛ.
[13] F I:205, 211. There are notes on the Psalms in F
I:207ᵛ; Q II:10-15; etc.   [14] Q IV:459.   [15] F I:49.

most obscure part of Holy Scripture, but also the most useful, the most pleasing, the most necessary for the interpretation of all the rest of the Bible. Study the Psalms from the Hebrew, if not for your own sake, then in order to help me. If you devote intense effort to it at first, you will be spared tedious difficulties later on. Of course we have St. Jerome's Psalter *secundum hebraicam veritatem*, but I think that a word for word study of the original can clarify a great deal. . . . How sweet it is to read the Psalms! It is not tiresome, but most delightful. What could I do that would please me more? In the Psalms I praise and glorify my Creator; I invoke, honor, and entreat Him; in the Psalms I thank Him and bless Him; in the Psalms I confess my sins and implore mercy; in the Psalms I consider the vanity of the world and the falsity of all things; in the Psalms I see myself mirrored and I understand the frailty of life, the paltry value of this mortal body, the danger of being carried far from God if the soul submits to the tyranny of the senses. The Psalms prove how noble the soul is if it profits by true self-knowledge instead of sinking to the level of the animals. And finally, in the Psalms I glimpse, insofar as the countless defects of my eyes permit, the infinite power, wisdom, and goodness of God. . . . If men studied the Psalter as eagerly as they study the sonnets of Petrarch or the Odes of Horace, they would find far more poetic charm in them—to say nothing of higher qualities—than in

Horace. Only those who have never given any close attention to the Psalms could say otherwise, just as there are people who understand nothing of Petrarch and therefore judge that his poetry is nonsense (which it really is!). But for me the Psalms are my only sonnets, my only odes!

"I learn them by heart so that I can say them without having to hold the book. The literal sense by itself pleases me so well, I find in them thought so high and so divine that I have not yet desired to look up the commentaries that find spiritual and allegorical interpretations. Perhaps some day I shall study them thoroughly, but for the time being I am satisfied with the literal sense. There I perceive what intense zeal filled David's heart and how far advanced he was in self-knowledge and self-contempt, that is, contempt of the mortal part of his being. This, in turn, brought him true knowledge and contempt of the world. Often I muse: "how mistaken are those who honor Homer among the Greeks, Virgil among the Romans, or Petrarch amongst us more than David, that most admirable Jew who has given us all the exquisite loveliness of poetry, all the nobility and subtility of true philosophy, all the tender feelings of a man enamored of true, eternal, heavenly beauty. We can, moreover, find in the Psalms such exact prophecies of Jesus Christ that we might well believe that some of them were composed after, rather than before His death, so explicitly does the literal sense refer to Him. I love to learn the Psalms by heart so that I can say them without effort, unhindered by illness or any other obstacle."[16]

David deserves our admiration because he experienced in advance all the sentiments of a Christian and especially the hermit's attitude of detachment from the world and yearning for God.[17] We should find Psalm 118 particularly thrilling, for it contains the sublime mysteries of Christ and all the doctrine necessary for our perfection.[18] A love of the Psalms is the mark of a true monk. Woe to those who scorn them! *Vae illis qui psalmos spernunt!*[19] On the other hand, those who admire them and receive them willingly find spiritual satisfaction in them. "The main concern of monks should be to bemoan their sins, to praise God for His infinite mercy towards them, and, with hearts overflowing with love, to cling to Jesus who hangs naked and bleeding on the Cross. It follows, therefore, that no physical or spiritual occupation can offer them greater satisfaction than the recitation of the Psalter. In the Psalms they can confess their sins and ask God's pardon, often in words so touching that the soul is roused to deep emotion. In the Psalms they praise and glorify our eternal Creator and Redeemer, perhaps more wonderfully than in any other part of Scripture."[20]

"We may well doubt whether any spiritual exer-

---

[16] F I:40. [17] Q I:51. [18] Q III:151.
[19] F II:105ᵛ. [20] F I:155.

cise can please the man who is bored by the Psalter. So suited is psalm-reading to monks that in former times when they made their profession they used to be urged to keep the Psalms always in their hands or on their lips. This meant that whenever a monk was free of other duties, the best thing he could do was to read the Psalms. . . . Nothing is more useful to monks, who in solitude and silence desire always to meditate, frequently to pray, and at times to attain contemplation."[21]

---

[21] Q IV:257.

X.

MENTAL PRAYER WITHOUT A METHOD

Study and psalmody are already genuine forms of prayer to the extent that they include attentive and thoughtful reading of Holy Scripture. For monastic prayer comprises three inseparable elements which the whole tradition affirms to be indispensable: *lectio, meditatio, oratio.* This concept of the life of prayer is recalled in the Rule of 1520. "All who know how to read will read Holy Scripture at least once a day. . . . But it is useless to read unless one also meditates on what is read with all possible devotion. Therefore, during the times of silence each one shall reflect upon what he has read while he is in his cell or at work. During the time when silence is broken to allow the brothers the recreation of fraternal conversation, they will speak of their reading. So they will avoid idle words and will make progress in the understanding of Scripture. But without God's help, reading and meditation would be of no avail, just as all other observances would be likewise impossible. We must, therefore, give first place to mental prayer: for the main characteristic of a hermit is that he spends his time in prayer. While our fathers have not assigned any definite time of the day or night for mental prayer—as is done in other religious congregations —they meant thereby to indicate that continual prayer is as necessary to the spiritual life as breathing is to physical life. And so the hermits, whenever they have no other assigned task, should always pray. Each one will choose the time best suited to him when he will remain motionless in mental prayer for at least half an hour, either all at once or divided into shorter periods. Even if at times his distracted mind cannot concentrate on prayer, he must not fail to devote to meditation the time that has been appointed, kneeling before a picture of Christ or taking up whatever other position helps devotion. He may be assured that the time he spends thus will be counted as prayer and if he perseveres, he will soon, with God's help, be able to meditate with delight.

"Those who come to the hermitage from secular life or from a monastery must be trained to mental prayer before all else, for if a man who has been properly instructed does not then devote at least half an hour daily to mental prayer, he cannot persevere in our life. It is as impossible to grow spiritually without mental prayer as it is to grow physically without food. Mental prayer truly strengthens the mind for study and reflection, while the latter in turn foster mental prayer. The three activities are mutually dependent and mutually helpful. A man is a hermit in name only if he does not devote himself daily to reading, to meditation, and to mental prayer."[1] Each of these three forms of prayer has its own characteristic feature: *studiosa lectio, ordinata meditatio, devota oratio*. Reading must be attentive, not superficial. Meditation is an effort to concentrate, requiring that the mind should not wander but should fix its attention on very specific dogmatic and moral considerations. Mental prayer proceeds from meditation and takes the form of a direct conversation with God and inspired by God. For here again the only master is the Lord. No book can teach us to speak to Him: only the Holy Spirit can suggest how we should adore God and lament our sins. We must remain supple to the influence of the Spirit. We must choose the time when the spirit is most tranquil and free;[2] then grace will do the rest. At times there will even be granted to us the gift of contemplation. The rhythm of this process, however, varies for each soul and according to the God-given talents of each. Happy are those who need but a brief reading and short meditations in order to attain a

---

[1] RVE f. 83-83ᵛ.   [2] Q III:52.

prolonged state of mental prayer! Happy are those who then become rapt in contemplation, that state proper to the angels and the blessed in heaven, but sometimes granted by Almighty God to those who, though possessing a human body, practice a perfection verging on that of the angels! Their nature is then raised beyond its own powers. Their spirit enjoys the delights of God. Happy are those whose nature sometimes suffers such violence! Happy are those who experience such rapture for a longer time, if indeed it *can* last long!"[3]

The most important form of prayer is mental prayer in the strict sense. Blessed Giustiniani has left us a beginning of a treatise on this subject. It is impossible to summarize it without distortion, for it contains what is better than mere theory: a demonstration.[4] Its fundamental principle is that "mental prayer has many different forms." We can never find two men who pray in exactly the same way, and each man's way of prayer varies almost every time he prays. It is, therefore, vain and superfluous to seek a method of mental prayer; but the best method is to pray without a method. The Holy Spirit is an incomparable master in this art and we need only let Him guide us without looking backwards to find out by what path He is leading us. Just as a ship cuts its way through the waters of the

---

[3] F VIII:2; cf. also Q IV *bis*:173.

[4] Fortunately the text has been published in *Vita cristiana*, Rivista ascetico-mistica, XIV (1942), p. 117-144.

ocean but leaves no trace of its wake, so the soul propelled by the Holy Spirit across the ocean of divine contemplation cannot, even by looking backward, see either the route it has followed or the point it has reached.

If then, we wish to present the method which follows no method but permits every way of prayer, we must first note that the word *prayer* is not limited to the usual notion of *requesting some favor of God*. Usually prayer is truer and more efficacious when we ask nothing whatever of Him. Thus we can say that each Psalm and each verse of every Psalm is really a prayer even though many of them ask nothing of God. St. Paul suggests to Timothy four kinds of prayer, of which only one means *request*: "This first of all, I ask: that petition, prayer, entreaty and thanksgiving should be offered for all mankind."[5] We gain more by thanking God for his benefits than by asking Him for them; we please Him more by acknowledging our wretchedness and His mercy than by requesting the help of His mercy to relieve our wretchedness. Let each one, then, freely cling to the way of prayer that attracts him. He need not follow any particular pattern of prayer, but should follow the Holy Spirit which will guide him now by one path, now by another.

It is true that there are ready-made prayers that

[5] I Tim. II:1.

we can say and recite, but that kind of prayer resembles reading more than mental prayer. In mental prayer the soul is "suspended in God" without depending on any printed text. The prayer that it exhales under the inspiration of the Holy Spirit, the cries and moans that it utters, perhaps even with the voice, constitute genuine mental prayer. To impose an order and method to follow would be to debase mental prayer to an act of reading, whereas normally the opposite would occur—reading should lead to prayer. We must repeat, then, that mental prayer is not subject to any method, except the method of preparatory discipline. Instead of seeking a system for mental prayer, it would be better to learn how much fervor, purity, and contrition should mark our prayer. Instead of tracing a method of prayer, it would be better to strive to reach that proper degree of fervor and purity. This does not mean that prayer lacks any definite form: man's finite spirit cannot grasp an indeterminate object. But the fact remains that the best way to pray is to follow no particular way or, in other words, to follow every way. Blessed Giustiniani declares that he states this principle because it corresponds with his own experience: "truth forces him" to speak as he does.

Since he was asked how he himself prays, these seven words summarize all his attitudes: "I adore, I honor, I thank, I appeal, I await, and I desire: but what must precede all this is the avowal of my misery and unworthiness. In these seven words I sometimes strive to confine the vast number of different ways of praying. I find each of the seven as vast and deep as an abyss where the spirit can endlessly advance. Each of them suggests so many thoughts and so many types and qualities of mental prayer that no spirit, however noble, could reach the end even throughout a whole long lifetime of prayer. We begin by admitting our own misery; then we address God to adore, honor, thank, invoke, entreat and desire Him. But we can also express other attitudes, such as praising God, blessing, glorifying, magnifying and exalting Him.

One example can prove the inexhaustible content of each of these words. Let us begin with the act that should precede and prepare all the others: confession. Should we wish to classify the many considerations suggested by this word, we could think first of man's natural unworthiness, then of that due to his own sins, finally of that caused by his negligences, his ignorance, his coldness, and his voluntary weakness. Here Blessed Giustiniani takes up more than ten pages to acknowledge his own unworthiness. This interminable act of true humility proves, better than any theory, how easy it is for a contemplative soul to speak constantly to the Lord. Nor can we convey the bittersweet quality of the gentle tears that form the accompaniment of this interior dialogue. The confession of sin suffices to keep the soul in God's presence: *sibi soli et Deo vacat.* Then there ensues the whole intimate dialogue of man's relationship to God: all mankind confesses its misery and receives the answer that God addresses to all men: the grace of salvation.

A meditation without any method and almost without any requests is possible; it exists. The only proof is the experience of those who practice it. We have the testimony of certain very long rhapsodies written by Giustiniani on various mysteries and various Biblical texts.[6] "Particular intentions" have no place in these pages overflowing with a fervor that never abates. The soul expresses its faith and its yearning for God. It interrupts its acts of adoration only to beg for one gift which is the Lord Himself. But could we say that such prayer, where there occurs no thought of other men, is a form of egotism? No, for it is accompanied by a very strong feeling for the Church, an intense awareness of the reality of the Communion of Saints,[7] a conviction "that we cannot save ourselves without doing everything possible for the salvation of others."[8] Blessed Giustiniani's attention is fixed

---

[6] For example: Q III:11: *Pii ad Sanctum Spiritum affectus*; F II:100: *Soliloqui sulla santissima Eucaristia*; Q II:51: Sulle parole: *Signor mio e Dio mio*; Q II:63: Sulle parole: *Perchè mi hai veduto Tommaso, hai creduto.*

[7] Cf. F I:40; F I:175; Q IV:235. Cf. also chapter 4, p. 050, and chapter 16, p. 0158. Consult also: *Un humaniste ermite*, op. cit. p. 52.

[8] A collection of patristic texts illustrating this truth is found in Q IV *bis*, :214.

on all the great causes which involve the whole Church, the conversion of Islam, the return of separated Christians, etc. These major intentions are the purpose of his life. From time to time he formulates them, just as he sometimes prays for his relatives, his friends, and his enemies.[9] But when he is absorbed in deep mental prayer, he is aware of nothing but the presence of God alone.

While Blessed Giustiniani left no method of mental prayer, yet he clearly perceived the difficulty that all methods attempt to remedy. Instead of trying to solve the problem by some deceptively easy procedure, he strove to grasp the roots of the matter. This he did in a treatise whose very title is an apt expression of the problem: "Why is it that the soul, though experiencing great joy in mental prayer, finds it so difficult to persevere in it, while the contrary is true of other actions?" The answer is as profound as it is original:

"I have often wondered why it is that the pleasure we remember experiencing in certain agreeable activities enables us to repeat them with ease and joy, while, in spite of the incomparably greater pleasure tasted in mental prayer, the soul returns to it with difficulty and trouble, almost with reluctance. Those who, at least once, have derived great pleasure from sensual passion, from the delights of the table, from lovely music, or enthralling specta-

---

[9] e.g.: Q IV:365.

cles, are attracted to these experiences by the memory of the pleasure they felt. But though our soul feels such great and intense pleasure in mental prayer, once it has advanced in God's friendship to a point where it begins to taste some part of divine reality, yet we continue to feel a repugnance that is both physical and spiritual on returning to prayer, and that occurs even after we have felt these delights many times.

"I, for one, can testify that I enjoy the pleasure of eating, especially certain foods, so much that even without the stimulus of hunger or the serving of special foods, I begin to eat so naturally and easily that I hardly notice what I am doing or pay any particular attention. But I have to do violence to myself, so hard do I find it to return to mental prayer, even though, thanks to our dear Lord Jesus Christ, the delights I have tasted therein more than once infinitely surpass all else that I have known. Indeed I do not ask this question through mere curiosity but in order to know and eliminate the reason that makes me postpone my mental prayer. I would like to be able to return to it as easily as I do the sensual acts that give me pleasure. As I pondered the question, several reasons have occurred to my mind. The first is that the soul is a noble substance, or in other words, a delicate and subtle substance, while the body is a common substance, of coarse and hard matter. It is not surprising, therefore, that the soul receives the impressions of the body more easily than the body those of the soul. Sensual pleasures arise in the body and proceed to the soul, which easily consents to them because it is instantly affected by them: hence its feeling of satisfaction when the body leads it towards some pleasure. On the contrary, the pleasure of mental prayer first affects the spirit, the part of the soul farthest removed from the body. Thus when the soul is stirred by the joy it has known in mental prayer and wishes to return to it, the body, which did not taste that pleasure, or at least did not retain the memory of it, refuses its consent to the soul. For we assent easily to all actions in which the body and the soul act with common consent. That doubtless explains why it is so easy to return to physical pleasures, where the soul offers no resistance to the body, but it is hard to return to the spiritual joy of mental prayer, where the body rebels against the soul. That very resistance is the cause of the difficulty.

Similarly, for instance, when we go walking: we find it easy to descend a mountain, because in this action the heavy nature of the body is in agreement with the soul's desire. But if, on the contrary, we wish to climb the mountain, the body's heavy nature feels such repugnance that the soul must do violence not only to the body but to itself because of its own reluctance to force the body. The same is true of mental prayer: the struggle the soul must undertake against the body is so unpleasant to both body and soul that both agree to flee from the joy of mental prayer. In like manner a man who well knows that a bitter medicine will restore his health, consents to take it, but only with the greatest repugnance, for the bitterness of the medicine repels not only the body but also the soul that is affected by the distaste our senses experience. So with mental prayer: while the soul, attracted by the memory of its joy, longs to return to it, nevertheless, because this return is an assault on the body, a separation of body and soul, a kind of death, the soul keenly feels this violence against the body. As its displeasure preceding mental prayer is stronger than its memory of the joy therein, it resists its own impulse. In order to avoid the displeasure that precede mental prayer, it no longer strives to attain the pleasure to be experienced during the actual time of mental prayer.

The contrary is also true: at times we refrain from immediate pleasure because of the distress that will result. Thus a man who rubs a wound that is almost healed feels great relief, but as he knows that an increase of pain will result if he reopens the wound permanently, he refrains from rubbing it. Many persons who would like to eat honey because it is sweet, find that it causes them stomach pains and therefore they deprive themselves of present pleasure because of future pain. So before mental prayer the prospect of a kind of separation of soul and body distresses the body, and through it also the soul, so much that prayer is forsaken because present pain, even though slight, makes a stronger impression than the image of future joy, even if it be much more intense.

I may add also that our attraction towards corporal pleasures is a purely natural attraction and whatever is according to nature is done easily because neither body nor soul feel it repugnant. On the other hand, our special attraction to the spiritual joy of mental prayer is not natural. I do not mean that it is contrary to nature, but that it is above nature. For the soul cannot practice mental prayer by its own strength alone, but it must be drawn to it by a special gift of God, an impulse coming directly from Him each time. As both body and soul are incapable of achieving this of their own accord, it contains an element of force. That is another reason why it is difficult to start mental prayer, though once started, great joy results.

But I think that the main reason of this difficulty is lack of practice. Even easy actions seem hard through lack of practice, while difficult actions become easy and pleasant for those who make them a habit. Thus all day long I am busy reading or writing and I do this with joy, without any repugnance because I am accustomed to it. To a person without this habit it would seem hard and almost intolerable. Similarly through force of habit we find it easy to keep seeking corporal pleasures which are always at hand; but we find it hard to remain true to the spiritual activity of mental prayer, just because we are not sufficiently accustomed to it. A maxim of pagan philosophers states that men should choose the more perfect way, even if it be more painful, because habit will make it easy. I am convinced that whatever the difficulty or its cause may be, there is no better, stronger, or more effective remedy to counteract it than constant practice. Habit makes the soul alert and able to control the body. The divine influence which first seemed oppressive becomes, as it were, connatural. The joy that we experience, no longer by anticipation but actually present here and now, exerts a stronger attraction as it lessens the distress we feel in establishing the habit.

In conclusion I shall say that the greatest obstacle to spiritual activity and the greatest difficulty in mental prayer is lack of practice. Nothing makes us so ready and eager for it as habitual practice. If you wish to pray easily, you must pray assiduously. If you want to taste the joy of mental prayer, make a habit of it and you will be overwhelmed with joy. Of course we should not pray merely because of the pleasure it gives us, but the pleasure is a means of coming closer to God, attributing everything to His glory, devoting ourselves more completely to His love."[10]

---

[10] Q IV *bis*: 173. Published in *Vita critiana,* Rivista ascetico-mistica XXI (1952), p. 149-156.

PART FOUR

The Hermit's Asceticism

XI.

THE INNER STRUGGLE

The hermit's asceticism is wholly determined by his life itself. Since he is trying to live with God alone, he must achieve radical detachment from all that is not God. He must attain the only true solitude, that of the spirit. This interior stripping is hard and must be safeguarded by constant effort. "Only one thing is hard: to tame the spirit, to force it to abandon the world really and truly, in deed and in heart. We must not be anxious to see our relatives or friends, to hear news of the world. We must be like Melchisedech, without father, mother, brother, friends, or country—free of all connection with things of this world. We must leave the world and live for the Creator alone."[1]

To some extent such interior detachment is re-

---

[1] F + :145.

quired of every monk, but it is harder for the hermit than for others because his very solitude makes him always vulnerable to that subtle enemy: self-love. Blessed Giustiniani denounces the danger with ruthless lucidity. "Man's whole life is an arduous, unrelenting struggle and we should be keenly aware of this dramatic inner conflict. Each part of man, the flesh and the spirit, struggles against the other and against itself. The flesh is in conflict with itself: discomfort is involved if we sleep, eat, and drink sparingly—but also if we sleep, eat, and drink abundantly. If we cater to the body, we risk injuring it; if we treat it severely, we run the same risk. No matter what is done for it, it voices a protest, so hard is it to find the golden means of its true needs. Even supposing this balance to be achieved, there will still remain the struggle of the flesh against the spirit because their aims are opposed to each other. The flesh delights in splendid mansions and vast estates; the spirit seeks a tiny cell with a little garden, knowing that poverty is the safer path to peace on earth and happiness in heaven. The flesh is fond of pleasure and sensual gratification, which the spirit avoids. It is the same in all things, for every aspiration of the spirit is opposed by the flesh. Constantly and in every sphere of activity, the struggle must be sustained. But it becomes relatively easy, in proportion as the spirit succeeds in dominating the flesh and keeping it in submission.

"There is, however, a still harder conflict, which

never abates: the hidden struggle of the spirit against itself. The spirit becomes its own enemy and insidiously attacks itself. It often sets up false values which appear genuine and which conceal all too well their harm. If we do good, we spoil it by self-satisfaction. If we practice mortification, we remember to summon prudence as a pretext to relax our ascetic efforts. How often the spirit tells lies to itself to try to deceive itself! For instance, if we yield to anger or impatience, we persuade ourselves that the motive is the service of God or charity towards our neighbor whom we wish to correct. In short, the spirit disguises vices as virtues until it no longer distinguishes one from the other: it cheats itself. Whenever it aims at a good purpose, such as the contemplative life, it manages to convince itself that some other purpose is better, such as helping others in the active life. It even seeks arguments against itself in Holy Scripture. Thus we should always distrust ourselves for we are always at odds with ourselves. We are exposed to illusions that we ourselves fashion. The greater our progress in good, the fiercer this interior war becomes. Indeed so greatly must we fear the ambushes that we set for ourselves that the only escape is in depending on the advice of another."[2] Only severe asceticism, controlled by strict obedience can save us from these dangers. The hermit's principal guarantee

---

[2] Q IV *bis*: 129.

against the illusion that the contemplative life can be easier than active life is its austerity. A more perfect life must be a more rigorous life. "You who have embraced the perfect and exalted life of hermits with God's help, must practice very severe austerity. Nothing less than excellence, even absolute perfection, is expected of you."[3] Hermits are distinguished from cenobites chiefly by their greater severity of life. As eremitic life is a stage beyond cenobitic life, more is required of the hermits than of the cenobite. For him the practices of cenobitic life represent a bare minimum to which he must always add in order to do better: *arctiora et perfectiora*.[4] All eremitic asceticism is a putting into practice in every detail this fundamental principle.

The best training in austerity consists in first depriving ourselves of all pleasure. If life is hard, then things that others find austere may seem pleasing to us, and what would be unbearable in a life of ease will cause but little suffering.[5] The first way to restrain the natural appetite for pleasure is privation and we must begin with the appetite for food, that is, we must fast. "The food must be cheap, plain, and scarce; the drink must be weak and meager. Your one meal a day must be preceded by a blessing of the food, accompanied by reading, followed by a prayer of thanksgiving. You must not advance the

---

[3] Q III:245.   [4] RVE f. 44ᵛ, 54ᵛ, 108, 109, etc.
[5] Q I:62.

time of meals or care about the quality of the food or increase the quantity. Strive mainly to moderate your desire to eat, taking what is necessary and getting rid as quickly as possibly of this need to eat."[5a]

Similar directions are given on other points: "Sleep briefly but for as long as nature demands. . . .[6] Your bedding should not include the fine linen that cenobitic monks sometimes use.[7] Your clothing must be cheap, coarse, shabby—just a few plain and simple garments, nothing beyond what is strictly necessary."[8] The hair shirt and the discipline will be used, but always with modesty.[9] "If you cannot take the discipline without being heard by your neighbor, then have no scruples to dispense with it. Each of you may, if he wish, wear the hair shirt either always or only at certain times. But those who do not wish it will not be obliged to wear it."[10]

Thus mortification must always be controlled by prudence which is "the seasoning of all virtues," *omnium virtutum condimentum.*[11] Prudence does not excuse us from austerity, as a certain subtle egoism may often try to maintain. On the contrary it safeguards austerity against the excesses of self-love and self-satisfaction. It keeps austerity in its proper place in the hierarchy of means of sancti-

---

[5a] Q III:52.   [6] Q III:52.   [7] RVE f. 108ᵛ.
[8] Q III:52.   [9] RVE f. 109ᵛ ff.
[10] Rule of 1524, Lugano edition, p. 159.
[11] RVE f. 110; cf. f. 95ᵛ, 97ᵛ, etc.

fication, preventing it from casting off the rule of the spirit.

Asceticism includes manual work, because it keeps the soul humble, even when it is not required as the way to earn a living. As hermits are striving to lead a more perfect life, it is all the more necessary for them: nothing can excuse them from it. "The cenobites often try to dispense with it, either because of the exertion of singing the Divine Office or because of the inconvenience of their location, if the monastery is situated in a city. But hermits can invoke neither the chant or the location as excuses."[12]

Finally, the best opportunities for mortification are those we do not choose ourselves or create artificially. Cold weather, rain, and snow are inevitable in hermitages which had to be built on mountains in order to assure isolation. We should cheerfully accept the bad weather: we have frequent opportunities to bear it as our cells are not connected with the Oratory by a roofed-in cloister, as in the Charterhouse. During the long winters, before each liturgical service by day or by night, we should face the bad weather "for the love of Christ."[13] Blessed Giustiniani often refers to the cold. In his personal notes he has even sketched the outline of a meditation on the Christian acceptance of cold weather. "To support the cold, remember that

---

[12] RVE f. 99ᵛ-100.   [13] RVE f. 64ᵛ.

Christ was born in the Winter; he was clothed only in poor swaddling bands; he wam warmed only by the breath of animals in a stable because there was no room for Him at the inn. He was crucified naked, also in a cold season on a hill exposed to the wind. Do you want the proof that it was cold even in the city, even in a house, even for those who were clothed? Read what the Gospel says: "It was cold, and the servants and officers had made a charcoal fire, and stood there warming themselves."[14] Just think, then, of how cold the naked body of Jesus must have been on Calvary. Remember how it is told that St. Maurus used to go out half-clothed in winter in order that he could suffer from the cold. Think of the martyrs who died by the torture of freezing: in the readings assigned for the Feast of All Saints we learn that many of the saints were tortured by the cold."[15]

Thus we see that the hermit's asceticism does not involve extraordinary mortifications, but requires above all an acceptance of the mortifications of everyday life, a joyful acceptance. The word most frequently used to indicate how the hermit is to fulfill his duties is an adverb that is hard to translate by a single word. *alacriter.*[16] The hermit should accept the observances of his austere life with zest, enthusiasm, eagerness. He should be gay. The

---

[14] John 18:18.   [15] F II:125.
[16] F A:22ᶜ, 22ᵃ. RVE f. 42, 43, 43ᵛ, 100ᵛ, etc.

happy peace of his soul should be evident from the relaxed features of his cheerful face.[17] He should possess and radiate the gift of joy, *iucunditas*.[18] His whole life has but one purpose: "to serve God voluntarily in a more perfect way, for the love of Christ with spiritual joy."[19]

---

[17] RVE f. 7.   [18] RVE f. 71ᵛ.
[19] Prologue to the Rule of 1524, Lugano edition, p. 136.

XII.

DESTITUTION

"The eremitic observances and rules contain no perfection in themselves and are means whereby we may attain the perfection of the evangelical and apostolic ideal."[1] This ideal comprises two essential elements: to love one another and to renounce everything in order to be poor, following the footsteps of Christ who was poor. The fact that hermits live together gives them the opportunity to practice both fraternal charity and poverty. But their eremitic ideal imposes on them the duty of accepting the most rigorous implications of utter poverty which should be one of the characteristic features of their life. Poverty of spirit and interior detachment are a natural consequence of their vocation. Since hermits leave the world in order to live with

---

[1] RVE f. 43ᵛ.

God alone, they should abandon everything that belongs to the world and every desire to possess anything in this world. "In the use of those things necessary to support human weakness, the hermits should be satisfied with whatever is plainest and cheapest and they should be on guard against any desire for possession or any attachment to the things they use. So they will truly live the eremitic life according to the apostolic ideal. Then they will be in the world as if they were not in it and they will use the things of this world as if they were not using them. Even if many things are lacking, no one should worry about it very much or even wonder secretly: "What shall we eat! What shall we drink? What shall we wear?" But they will put all their trust in God, relying on these words uttered by the mouth of Truth Himself: "Seek first the kingdom of God and His justice and all these things shall be given to you."[2]

Extreme poverty is also appropriate to another characteristic of the hermit life: simplicity. The hermit suppresses all artificial needs; he eliminates the superfluities which for many people become necessities. By breaking all connection with the world in order to live with God alone, he reduces his needs to the fewest basic essentials; he is satisfied, we might say, with a bare minimum. So it is that his poverty coincides with his simplicity, his charac-

---

[2] F A:7.

teristic purity of life: *eremitica puritas*.[3] It is very appropriate to the humility of his state of life, for while the hermit life in the Church is conducive to the highest perfection, yet in the hierarchical order it is the lowest state of all. Since the hermit is separated from men, he has no right to any role in the government of the state and of the Church: he belongs to the lowest class of society, among the poor. He should live like them and consider himself one of them. For him to become a prelate would be a betrayal.[4] He must ever avoid comparing his life with that of other religious and only in case of necessity will he describe the manner of life of the hermitage.[5] When he is travelling and stays in a cenobitic community, he should do the most menial tasks, which are best suited to the humility of his state.[6] If he is the Superior of the hermitage, he should put himself last among the brethren. He will take his share of the necessities of life only after he has served all the others, beginning with the last: the leftovers will be for himself.[7]

Detachment, simplicity, humility are but different names for the same poverty of spirit. The hermit who possesses these qualities will find no difficulty in practicing material poverty. It includes two related duties: first, to possess nothing of our own, but to receive and to use according to our needs a part of what the community possesses; secondly, to ac-

---

[3] F A:6ᵛ.   [4] RVE f. 42.   [5] RVE f. 60.
[6] RVE f. 107ᵛ.   [7] RVE f. 127ᵛ.

cept the fact that the community itself should have few possessions for little would it avail us to renounce all personal property, if a rich community then provided us with resources which we would probably never have enjoyed otherwise. The first requirements of religious poverty are: to possess nothing of our own, not to appropriate to ourselves any of the goods of the community, not to use things as if we owned them, to keep things in the same state as when they were entrusted to us, to be always willing that things be taken away from us. The Rule of Eremitic Life not only contains practical rules in this regard but it also points out the meaning of the rules. If, for example, the hermit is forbidden to have any key except that of the Church, it is to teach him that nothing belongs to any one person. It will only be entirely evident that the hermits possess nothing of their own but that everything is for common use when they no longer need keys: "nothing that is for the use of all should be locked up."[8] You should leave at the library a written list of the books you have taken out: that is not only for the sake of good order, since it is important to be able to find the volumes, but also because they belong to everyone and should be at everyone's disposal.[9]

The second condition of true poverty is that the community itself be really poor. It should avoid

[8] RVE f. 53ᵛ.   [9] RVE f. 54.

acquiring anything beyond a bare minimum of possessions. It should not seek to receive legacies or
donations. When a young man of wealth announced
his intention of entering the hermitage and be-
queathing his possessions to it Blessed Giustiniani
answered him thus in the name of all the brethren:

"We are ready to consent to this desire which
you express. . . . I must tell you that you will find
many weaknesses among us, for we are men and we
are sinners. Our way of life is that best suited to
sinners and penitents: we would not want you to
ignore the fact that it includes many austerities.
But nothing is so hard or troublesome that it does
not become easy to those who rely on God's help
rather than their own strength. As to your desire
to give us part of your possessions, it is praiseworthy, but you must understand that we do not consider these riches as true riches. We do not prize
earthly treasures, which we have rejected once and
for all for the sake of Christ's love. We do not seek
that kind of profit: we seek primarily God's glory
and the salvation of souls. Therefore, dear brother,
we welcome you yourself, not your possessions.
If we receive you it is not in order that we may
become richer through your riches, for we wish to
remain poor. It is in order that you, by becoming
poor with us, and by bearing the yoke of obedience
may walk in the footsteps of Christ who was poor
and naked, and may thus more easily acquire eternal riches. . . . We hope to see you arrive in our

midst full of virtues, not laden with gold and silver.
. . . Whether you bequeath your wealth to us or
to other servants of Christ who are still poorer than
we are, you may be sure that you will gain much
by leaving all things in order to follow Christ."[10]

Blessed Giustiniani has often spoken of poverty
and one of his most constant concerns was to preserve genuine poverty in the hermit life. He did not
write a particular treatise on the subject, as he did
on many other points. But in this domain more than
in any other the facts are the strongest testimony. Instead of presenting a theory of poverty Giustiniani
has described the poor life of his hermitages at a
time when they were very close to the ideal he has
set up. Here are some extracts from this impressive
text:

"As to the life of the hermits, my fathers and
my brothers, I shall tell you only the most ordinary
and most evident facts. . . . As to food, they unfail-
ingly observe the fasts of the hermitage of Camaldoli and keep other even more severe fasts. . . . I
do not think that in the four hermitages during the
course of a year, we have eaten more than about a
hundred eggs: most of our hermits abstain from
eggs as strictly other monks of perfect observance
abstain from meat. During the last two years, some
of the hermits were ill from time to time, but none
ate meat: they had only a few eggs. In one her-

[10] F VII:103.

mitage where five fathers were living, they ate only seven eggs during the year. Most of them abstain from fish also. Some have tasted eggs and fish only two or three times in two years, and that because of guests. . . . Usually their food consists of hard bread or moldy bread. One of the fathers asserts that in one of the hermitages of which he had charge there was some of this moldy bread and it was served to the donkey who refused it—but the hermits ate it! I myself have seen that in two hermitages when the bread was put on the table (for sometimes before the cells were built the hermits ate together) each one tried to get the bread that was most moldy. Besides bread, they eat vegetable soups. But do not imagine that they cook a meal every day: at times I have eaten for four successive days beans that had been cooked all at one time. Garlic, or scallions, or fruit make up a real treat. They find boiled acorns as tasty as chestnuts: I have even learned to eat and enjoy them. The fact of the matter is that on some days they do no cooking because they find in the forest food that requires no preparation. . . . Their clothing is as poor and shabby as possible: the tunic a bit more than calf-length, with a scapular reaching a little below the knee and undergarments like sacks: pieces of cloth in front and back, but not sewed at the sides. I do not think that more than two or three of them wear stockings; the others wear none. Moreover some wear clogs, like those of St. Francis, only during the winter. In the summer they go barefoot. During the last two years I have learned to walk without stockings and this year I shall try to wear the clogs with nothing else. So far I have felt the cold less than when I wore stockings. . . . I once had to buy all the clothing for one of the hermits: for everything—undergarment, tunic, scapular, and cloak—I spent at the most fourteen coppers. The cincture is merely a rope. . . . The hermits have only one tunic and few of them have two undergarments. . . ."[11]

Unfortunately this description of the life of Giustiniani's first companions was left incomplete. What was written is none the less valuable. Doubtless this heroic period could not last forever. But it remains as a symbol of a vocation that included destitution, because God alone suffices.

---

[11] *Re.* the circumstances in which this text was written cf. *Un humaniste ermite*, op. cit. p. 118-120.

XIII.

PERFECT OBEDIENCE

Unlike poverty, obedience was dealt with by Giustiniani in a long and explicit treatise.[1] Real destitution, when voluntary, is the proof of interior detachment—if the former is present, we know that the latter has been attained. But the virtue of obedience is an interior attitude which is not so clearly evident in practice. Like poverty of spirit, it too abides in the soul; unlike poverty, it has fewer opportunities for exterior expression. In a well-regulated community, it is even possible that a life of apparent submission might be devoid of obedience. Giustiniani, therefore, felt obliged to emphasize the qualities required to make obedience perfect.

---

[1] There are several versions of it. Here we quote from the edition published by Dom N. A. Giustiniani, O.S.B.: *Trattato dell' Ubbidienza del B. Paolo Giustiniani,* (Padua, 1753). The treatise is also summarized in RVE, chaps. XI-XII, f. 55ᵛ-60.

Many times he asserted the primacy of obedience in the life of monks, and more particularly, of hermits. The great originality of Camaldolese eremitic life is, in his eyes, that it reinstates in eremitic life the obedience proper to cenobitic life. Obedience is the virtue that makes a monk. Without it, the cenobite can live in his monastery as in a prison. Without it, the solitary resembles a wild animal more than a Christian hermit. What makes us monks and hermits is neither the cloister nor the solitude, nor even all the other virtues together: it is perfect obedience.[2] It belongs to both cenobites and hermits, and the treatise dealing with it is only a commentary on the references to it in the Rule of St. Benedict. Here again, however, the hermit life is more rigorous than any other way of life and it permits no mediocrity. And so, in order to point out the heights of renunciation to be scaled by any religious seeking to be perfect, he undertakes a subtle analysis of what we might call the psychology of obedience. He maps out in detail its whole path of progress, or as he says, its degrees. Here is his own summary of the subject:

"The first step is to banish all tardiness in our obedience: we learn to obey immediately, without any delay. Then we learn to drop what we were doing, even if it is something necessary to us. The

[2] Op. cit. 6-7.

third degree teaches us to leave unfinished what we were doing. Fourthly, we no longer are concerned about what we do and we renounce continuing it, either now or later, if obedience prevents us. The fifth step is the desire that we may always receive commands that will provide an opportunity to drop what we are doing. The next step eliminates all reluctance and feelings of fear in troublesome, difficult, or dangerous matters that we are commanded to undertake. The seventh degree precludes all delay or discouragement during the performance of what is commanded, for one can begin eagerly and then slow down through negligence, when the task imposed is time-consuming, tiring, or seemingly unreasonable. Eighthly, we are set free of all lukewarmness or coolness that can occur in the begnning, in the middle, or at the end of obedience. The ninth and tenth degrees curb all exterior and interior complaining. In all these stages we rise above the imperfections that menace obedience; we purify it of every possible taint. But we have not yet attained perfect obedience which begins only when we obey with spiritual joy—that is the eleventh degree. Finally, obedience reaches its twelfth and last degree of perfection when it is practiced with an upright intention, purified of all vain glory, hypocrisy, or false ambition—when we seek neither to appear virtuous nor to be praised, but only to please Jesus Christ. Pure love of Christ enables us to obey no longer like servants, but like sons of God."[3]

This scale of twelve degrees is necessarily somewhat artificial. But it provides the occasion for many shrewd and accurate observations. Examples of practical obedience are found in the actual life of the hermits. "Suppose that a monk has settled in a corner of the Church to say a certain number of Our Fathers. If the Superior summons him, he will be willing to interrupt his prayers, without completing the intended number of Our Fathers, even if there are just a few left to say. But he must even be ready to interrupt the Our Father that he had begun. If only the Amen remained to be said, and he consciously persisted in saying it before heeding his superior's order, that monk would not have obeyed perfectly. . . .[4] Every year at the haying season we hermits are sent out for two or three consecutive days to pitch the hay that has been mown by the peasants. If a certain monk is sent there and goes without delay, he has reached the first stages of obedience. But he has scarcely begun the haying when he is overcome by the heat or by fatigue. If he goes to sit down or stroll about in the shade of the forest, instead of persevering in the work he has been ordered to do, then he has not obeyed perfectly."[5]

---

[3] *Ibid.* chaps. XVIII-XX, p. 129-135.
[4] *Ibid.* p. 46.   [5] *Ibid.* pp. 95-96.

With regard to interior dispositions, the demands of perfect obedience are boundless. "St. Benedict says that the monk should surrender his own will: that means that we should abandon all wish, concern, or desire for the work we were doing, when the superior's order removes us from it. Now it is easier to interrupt physically the work we have begun than to become really detached from it. The will imposes its rule upon the body as upon a servant. But the mind, the imagination, and the emotions submit less easily to the control of the will. But they too, along with the body, must withdraw from the work they began, when it is interrupted by a command."[6]..."It is not even sufficient to obey when the order is given; if it is not given, we should desire it and take pleasure in expecting it. Of course the monk cannot actually keep his mind continually fixed on this specific desire, but it must be an habitual state, so that a decision he has taken once and for all keeps him always eager to accept a command that obligates him to abandon whatever he enjoys doing. It is not hard to obey promptly if we are doing nothing in particular, nothing that we find interesting or urgent: then it is even a pleasure to be punctual. But it is quite the contrary when we must interrupt work that we do gladly and find interesting."[7] The spirit of obedience means not merely a passive state, a certain readiness to receive

---

[6] *Ibid.* pp. 56, 59.   [7] *Ibid.* pp. 64-65.

orders. It takes the positive step of welcoming beforehand all opportunities for renouncement, accepting them before they even occur.

When an order is given the obedient monk carries it out without argument. "He submits like a beast of burden that does not strive to examine the load he is carrying on his back; he ignores whether the pack he hauls be useful or not. Be it gold or manure—both are accepted in the same way. Moreover, the animal does not enquire whether it is being led by the direct path or by a detour: it follows the road its driver sets."[8] Nor is it enough to obey without protest, for exterior silence is fruitless without interior peace. Placidity can become mere withdrawal if the spirit refrains from resisting but refuses its active consent. We must submit without strain, complaint, or regret; in fact our obedience should even be easy, supple, and happy. Only then, as St. Benedict says, does it become really pleasing, acceptable to men and to God.[9] "Obedience should be accompanied by real spiritual joy, eager delight, cheerfulness, holy contentment. Of course we do not mean the mere natural pleasure we may feel if what is commanded suits our own tastes, desires, and intentions. In that case we cannot call it a spiritual joy, even if what is commanded seems to foster the good of our soul. But to make our joy supernatural rather than natural we must rejoice all the

---

[8] *Ibid.* p. 110.   [9] *Ibid.* p. 115.

more in proportion as that which is commanded is the more contrary to our own personal tastes."[10]

The treatise on obedience concludes with a long contemplation of Jesus Christ, the model of perfect obedience. "We should fix our gaze always on the shining example of the Lord who declared that his food was only to do the will of the Father. Similarly the food of religious souls is found only in doing the will of the superiors. He who is not nourished by this food can neither advance nor even persevere in religious life, even if he possessed all the other virtues. The body cannot subsist or grow unless it is nourished: otherwise to apply all sorts of ointments or to cover it with precious clothing is of no avail. So also a monk's soul, even if adorned with all the gifts of the Holy Spirit, cannot grow in perfection if it lacks the bread of obedience. And souls that do not wish or seek this bread, who do not relish it when it is offered to them, or who eat it without a hearty appetite, are weaklings and resemble sick men who can no longer savor the bread which healthy men enjoy so much. Obedience is the bread that, as the Bible says, strengthens the heart of man. Each of us, therefore, should often repeat to himself: 'I want to seek no other food but to do the will of my superior so that I may follow the Lord who, by obeying His eternal Father in all things, has provided for me the living

---

[10] *Ibid.* pp. 124-125.

example of perfect obedience. He who was God, the eternal Word, equal to the Father, took on the form of a slave: through obedience He deigned to become the Son of Man and to be born of the Virgin Mary. . . . Through obedience He accepted hunger, sleep, vigils, fatigue, all the trouble that is common to all men. Besides that, He also suffered extreme poverty, exile, the oppression of the crowds that so pursued Him that it is recorded in St. John's Gospel that He had not enough time to eat His bread. He did not refuse to bear the hatred of the chief priests, the scribes, and the pharisees, as well as temptations from the devil and from men. He was not worried by the persecutions inflicted on Him by the very men to whom He had come, in obedience to His Father, to proclaim the Gospel. In spite of the detractions and insults heaped upon Him, He did not delay in the task He had to accomplish for the salvation of men. He never answered except with words wholly gentle and meek. He endured the ingratitude of His own people, the ingratitude of His country, the ingratitude of the throngs to whom He served the bread of eternal life and the bread of earthly life. He even bore the betrayal of the very men whom He had chosen in preference to all others—the treason of Judas and the denial of Peter, the desertion of all of them during the Passion. Finally He bore the suffering of being taken prisoner, being bound, insulted, hit, tortured, whipped, crowned with thorns, judged, condemned, crucified. From the Cross He heard abuse and blasphemy; He was given gall to drink. He wished to die like a lamb offered in sacrifice. His face remained serene; He did not complain; He simply said these words: 'Father, not my will, but Thine, be done.' Why, dear Jesus, did it please You to bear such pain, except because You wished to obey Your Father who sent You? You came to do His will: Your only food was to do the will of the Father."[11]

---

[11] *Ibid.* chapter XXII, pp. 140-151.

PART FIVE

Universal Love as the Ultimate Goal

XIV.

SELF-EFFACEMENT

Blessed Paul Giustiniani's teaching attains its goal and its glory in his mystical doctrine: to that all else is subordinate. The hermit life, the spiritual exercises, and the ascetical practices lack all sense and purpose if they do not lead to mystical union with God, a certain direct experience of God. In this real more than in any other, Giustiniani's teaching is linked to his own experience, and he expresses himself in long effusions which defy analysis. Even if we can summarize them exactly, we cannot translate their tonality. Because of the intense fervor animating these texts, it is desirable that they should be the first to see publication. Since we cannot yet read them in print, let us at least try to describe the state of soul that they imply and the doctrine that they contain. Needless to say, the reality we are dealing with here is characterized by unity and simplicity: its fullness is involved in each of its aspects; its totality is included with each of its phases. For the sake of explanation we can distinguish various degrees or elements in it, but by doing so we detract from the whole. In our minds we must constantly rebuild the synthesis and restore its vital unity.

The fundamental attitude of the soul united to God is detachment from itself. When a soul lives habitually in this state of radical renouncement, then at times it is given a realization of its own nothingness. Keenly aware of its own helplessness, it plunges into the depths of God and receives all from His love. Blessed Giustiniani received the grace of experiencing, in an ineffable way that surpasses all explanation, that he was nothing without God. But he had merited this favor by his constant humility. We must, therefore, recall the basic principles that are the foundation and the preparation of this experience.

In speaking of the degrees of perfection as suggested by the beginning of Psalm 118, Blessed Giustiniani marks the first as self-knowledge. By sin the soul cleaves to the earth: *adhaesit pavimento anima mea.* In a certain sense it is dead and it asks for life: *vivifica me secundum verbum tuum.* Then it regrets its sins, chooses to do good, even to practice virtue "eagerly and easily, or rather, meekly and for love of God." Once this last point is reached, men can speak to God of having run in the way of His com-

mandments because He has enlarged their hearts."[1]
Thus the first condition of every conversion is
hatred of self and of sin: the path to humility is self-
knowledge. Giustiniani composed several prayers
where he begs for self-knowledge.

"Lord Jesus, you who are the light without
which nothing can be illuminated, you who alone
see the darkness of my life, I dare not ask you for
the light that may show me your light: it is enough
that you show me my darkness. I am so blind that
I cannot see it and I mistake it for light. I am so
deeply in error that I do not perceive my error: I
mistake falsehood for truth. Death has advanced
upon me so far that, covered with wounds and
sores, I no longer feel the pain of my wounds.
Bring me back to myself: for in my misery I have
strayed not only from You but also from myself;
I have become a stranger to myself. Bring me back
to myself in order that I may then go towards You.
Show me my darkness, so that I may then look at
the Light: if I am in ignorance of my own misery,
I cannot have recourse to Your mercy. Because of
my sins I am worth nothing in the eyes of Your
Majesty: grant that I may likewise be worth nothing in my own eyes also; grant that I may despise

---

[1] Q IV *bis*: 199ᵛ [These lines of the Psalm, in the Knox
translation, are: "Deep lies my soul in the dust. . . . Crown
thy servant with life, to live faithful to thy commands.
. . . Do but open my heart wide, and easy lies the path
thous hast decreed."—Tr. note.]

myself completely, that I may behold my utter impurity. I am nothing in Your eyes until I am brought to nothing in my own eyes. I cannot rise from my ruin as long as I do not see it. And so I do not say to You with Moses: 'Show thyself to me'; I only say: 'Show myself to me.' "[2]

"*Ostende meipsum mihi.* I, who cannot see myself, how could I see You? Nothing is nearer or more familiar to me than my own conscience: and yet so dense is the cloud that hides me from myself that I cannot see my sins. Daily, constantly, I fall into sin and error; I offend God and my neighbor: but at the very moment of my sin and error I am so blind that I forget what I am doing. All too often I neglect to do what You command or I do what You forbid: in every way I transgress Your commandments. Yet I am not conscious of breaking Your commandments, or if I am aware of my sin, I forthwith forget it. How can I confess my faults, as I am obliged to do, if I do not know them? And so I say, Lord, and I keep repeating: 'Show me to myself, that I may know my sins.' "[3]

This mysterious humility is not the morbid and self-centered complacence of those who cultivate feelings of guilt which they should discard. Humility, on the contrary, gives rise to trust in God. The deeper a man's misery is and the greater his awareness of his own misery, the stronger is his appeal to

---

[2] F + :201.   [3] Q III:160.

God and his hope in God. "The Lord, as one of the Psalms says, lifts up those who fall. I have fallen, Lord, and I continue to fall. I have departed far from You and far from myself and I wallow in vile pleasures. See what a mire of iniquity I have entered! If I depended upon myself alone, I could never rise from it. And if I considered my sins, I would hesitate to hope in God; but when I consider Your mercy, my hope knows no bounds. 'The Lord lifts up those who fall': behold, Lord, I have fallen; I am sinking deeper and deeper. Lift me up, Lord. Stretch out the hand of Your mercy to me. My fall has broken me, shattered me, soiled me. Who will pick me up, restore me, purify me? Who will bring back my innocence and tranquility? My soul, hope in the Lord; put your trust in Him, for He lifts up those who fall. Lift me up, Lord; I cling to my sins; my whole gaze is fixed on evil. But I am Your servant and Your creature: Your Son has redeemed me with His blood. Behold Your creature, stuck in the mire of iniquity, weeps as he begs You to fulfil the words of Your prophet, or rather of Your own Spirit: 'the Lord lifts up those who have fallen.' I never tire of repeating this promise which is the foundation of all my hope. I have fallen, Lord, but You are my God and my king: In Your almighty Majesty and infinite Goodness, lift me up that I may live again."[4]

---

[4] F + :233.

Self-knowledge is the essential condition for love of God: we must know our own worthlessness in order that we may cease loving ourselves and thus turn to God. For the wise men of pagan times, the peak of wisdom was self-knowledge. For Christians, that is only a beginning and for them even that very self-knowledge is more perfect than it was for the ancient philosophers. Christians know themselves as creatures dependent upon God and superior to all of material creation: this is their dignity. But they also know themselves as sinners who are separated from God: that is their abasement. Henceforth, abasement brings men the realization of their need of God; their abasement proves their inability to attain God by their own efforts. Should they, then, despair? Is there no solution? Christ is the solution; He is the way of our return to God. "Jesus Christ, true God and true man, removed all impediments. As man He has accepted the punishment due to men's sins; as God He has offered Himself to His Father on the wood of the cross. Now the debt is paid. We, who doubted that we could even know the inaccessible Creator, are now allowed to contemplate God made man, the Word made flesh. Christ descended to our humility so that by knowing it and loving it, He might lift us up to His sublimity. He lived among men in order that we might learn to live with God among men. He endured death—the most painful death—to teach us to love Him: He, who was able to rise again when

He pleased, could have come down from the cross. But He offered Himself for us willingly, freely. Now that our debt is paid, now that our souls have been purified in the font of baptism, there remains no obstacle to our ascent to God. Let us rise to the Father, through the Mediator between God and men. Christ's humanity gives us access to His divinity.

"True, even since the Incarnation, even since our baptism, our sins are countless and defile us utterly. But do they impede our approach to Christ? Are we condemned to die in despair? No, for God wills that sinners should be converted and should live eternally once they have done penance. There are two remedies to sin, two ways of being released from it: the virtue of penance and the sacrament of penance."[5] So it is that humility and self-knowledge form the foundation of all ascetical and sacramental life.

A long meditation "on the perfect and true path to salvation" should deserve full quotation. After ruthlessly denouncing the subtle self-love that separates us from God, the pride which erodes our hearts and viciates our best actions, Blessed Paul again proves that the only right road by which to return to God is humility, the humility that was perfectly exemplified in Christ. "Our hidden self-love brings forth all manner of illusions: ecstasies,

---

[5] F II:61.

visions, revelations, prophecies, abstinences impossible to human strength, the experience of Christ's sufferings such as the wound on the side or the stigmata, knowledge acquired without study, speaking in strange languages, the desire to be damned for the love of Christ, extraordinary seeking of humiliation, sublime confessions, fasting from all food except the Blessed Eucharist, vigils beyond human strength, unduly prolonged meditations, knowledge of others' secret thoughts, miracles, and cures. All these marvels are, in some instances, nothing but the work of him who said—and would like to induce us to say: 'I shall be like God,' and I shall do what He does. . . . I think that these saints inspired by Lucifer are much more numerous, or rather much better known and more admired by the world, than the true saints, who do nothing in order to be known by the world, but who prefer to remain hidden. Christ's true servants love God totally and themselves not at all. So sheltered are they by humility that they are known to God only, not to men." Of course we must not condemn all visions and marvels: some are authentic. But the touchstone that can test them is always humility, a participation in the humility of Jesus.

Christ is the model of absolute humility. It can be shown that Christ, in His human nature, practiced the greatest possible spiritual humility. First, because He did not claim as His own either His divine being or His heavenly doctrine or His miraculous power. Nor did He wish that men should attribute these privileges to Him, for He knew and He acknowledged that everything came to Him from the Father. He sought not His own glory but the glory of His Father. The second proof of Christ's humility is that He who was equal to the Father voluntarily took on the form of a slave. In all things except sin, He became united to that human nature which was in subjection to the devil. He, who was God, became man and assumed a true human nature. Finally, He did even more than assume human nature and human flesh: in His deep humility He also voluntarily accepted the weakness of that nature, though He could have been born exempt from all frailty. He willed to appear in the flesh—in the flash that is weak and subject to pain. Thus did He give us the true norm of perfect humility.

So it is that the key to humility is likewise the whole secret of the hermit life: God alone. Jesus Christ, as man, was perfectly humble because He did not love Himself, but adored and loved God in utter simplicity. He was not glorified in Himself, but in God alone. He humbled Himself in order that He might contemplate only His Father's glory: therein lay His only pleasure. By the light of Christ, therefore, we can definite spiritual humility: just as pride of the spirit (the pride of Lucifer and of those who accept his domination) consists of self-love and self-admiration, accompanied by satisfaction with this love and admiration, so also humility means loving God, contemplating God, adoring God, seeking satisfaction in Him and Him alone. Genuine, solid humility is nothing but this pure love of God in utter simplicity. Where such love dwells, no place remains for self-love."[6]

Blessed Paul Giustiniani habitually maintained this attitude of knowing himself and despising himself, while loving God to the exclusion of self. On one occasion he received the grace of an even keener realization of the demands of humility and of love for God. Towards the end of his life, on August 7, 1524, during the celebration of Mass, divine light revealed to him just what it means to die to self in order to live for God alone. That very day he took up his pen and began to write while still under the influence of this experience. He had understood the absolute nature of divine love, which permits no attachment whatsoever to anything created and which requires of man an absolute self-renouncement. And so he wrote at length about this "annihilation of the soul" referred to in a verse of the Psalms: *ad nihilum redactus sum et nescivi*.[7] Later he himself made an outline of that fervent rhapsody: He distinguishes four kinds of annihilation, two that are evil, two that are good.

---

[6] Q IV *bis*:134ᵛ.

[7] This text is the first of six "Argumentations" which altogether constitute the book entitled *Secretum meum mihi o dell' amor di Dio* (ed. Frascati, 1941), pp. 45-53.

By the first, the soul is "reduced to nought" but "does not know it" when it is in a state of sin but is not aware of its own wretchedness and has no desire to escape from it. By the second, the soul is "reduced to nought" but is aware of its state. It is still in sin but by God's grace it knows it and is beginning at least to wish to recuperate. By the third annihilation, the soul is "reduced to nothingness" and knows it. Filled with burning love of God, it no longer lives in itself, but in God alone, or rather God lives in it and it knows itself only in God. Finally, the soul is "reduced to utter nothingness" and "it does not know it," for its vehement love of God so transforms it in God that it no longer loves self for self, nor self in God, nor God in self, but only God in God. No longer does it know self in self nor in God. No longer does it know God in self, but only God in God."[8]

It would be vain and even dangerous to try to summarize the further developments of these themes which occur to a saint who has been overpowered by God. It is better to have recourse to the original text, recently published. The words that a mystic used to express his experience of God can seem exaggerated when taken out of their context, but we should accept them, for the experience transcends our concepts. Suffice it to know that they are used by a theologian who is at home in our language

---

[8] *Ibid. Schema o breve summa o argumento*, p. 19.

when he is describing the things we know but who gives free rein to his fervor when he speaks to God to thank Him for His gifts. Nor does he stray off into obscure realms of speculation: on the contrary, he keeps ever in close contact with the sacraments. He keeps returning to his starting point and the very source of his experience, the reality of Christ's Eucharistic Body. "And how can it be, my soul, that you become nothing, that you now are nothing in yourself, that God alone is in you, or rather, you are in God? This happens only by the power of that sacrament, of which I was the unworthy minister a short time ago. Oh, how precious a treasure is the doctrine that brings us this truth: when we eat food for the body, we are not transformed into it, but it is transformed into us; on the contrary, when we approach the divine table of the Body and Blood of Jesus Christ, we eat food that is not transformed into us, but which transforms us into itself. Then we depart from ourselves and we begin to exist in God."[9]

---

[9] *Ibid.* p. 50.

XV.

TRANSFORMATION

"Happy is the soul that attains self-annihilation, and being totally converted to God, lives not in itself, but in Christ, wholly absorbed in His love. Happier still is the soul that is consumed in such a blazing fire of love that it no longer possesses either itself or Christ, no longer even lives in Christ, but lives only because Christ lives in it. *"Vivo ego, jam non ego, vivit vero in me Christus."*[1] In three "argumentations" of his book Giustiniani tries to describe the transformation of souls that climb to such sublime levels. These pages are marked by noble thought and fervent piety, but are at times bewildering in their subtility.[2] Because this perfect state is ineffable, only those who experience it can truly

---

[1] *Ibid.* p. 54.

[2] These are Numbers II-IV of the "Argumentations" in the *Secretum meum mihi.*

know it. However, some idea of its nature can be indicated by repetitions, reflections, and symbols.[3]

A series of comparisons illustrate how the soul can live by God's love. In the first place, we know that the flesh does not live by its own power, but by the soul from which it receives life. (By itself the flesh is dead.) So also the soul, if it does not love itself, lives not by its own power, but in God. Then, advancing a step further, we can see, secondly, that the flesh lives neither by its own power nor by the soul, because the life by which it lives belongs neither to itself nor to the soul. We can say, on the contrary, that the soul lives in the flesh, gives itself to the flesh which thus receives that life by which it lives. So also the soul, when it grows in love, lives neither in itself nor in God, because it does not love itself either in itself or in God. But rather, God alone lives in it, because it does not love itself in itself or itself in God, but only loves God in Himself. If we then rise to a still loftier viewpoint, we see, thirdly, that the human soul lives because life lives in it. It does not live in itself, for the soul has no life in itself, as God has. Moreover it does not live by means of life, because it has no other life by which it lives except life itself: only life lives in it. In like manner the soul lives by love: but it does not live in itself, nor does it live in God, nor does God live in it. God alone lives in God,

---

[3] Cf. *ibid.* p. 66.

and the soul lives by the very fact that it is transformed in God, when it loves neither itself in itself, nor itself in God, nor God in itself, but only God in God.[4] These words "God in God" are a constantly recurring refrain, the clue to the whole mystery of hermit life: "God alone in God. *Solo Dio in Dio.*"

"God is love and if the soul dwells in love, God is in it and it is in His love, so that God becomes the all in all." To help us glimpse how the soul can thus be lost in God, be transformed in Him, without, however, losing its own identity, the author introduces another series of distinctions. In the first place, the human soul has two kinds of life: essential life, received from God who is life and the source of all life; the life of love, also received from God Who is love and the source of all love. Just as essential life comprises three degrees, so there are three stages of the soul's life of love. In its essence, the soul does not subsist in itself but in God, from Whom it receives its being; similarly the soul that loves exists not in itself, but in God, for it has no self-love. Likewise the soul lives neither in itself nor in God, for by itself it neither exists nor has in itself the life by which it lives in God: rather, God alone lives in it, for it lives only insofar as God, Who is life, gives Himself to it. Thus God lives in the soul;

---

[4] *Schema, ibid.* p. 19-20. This summarizes the second "Argumentation"; *ibid.* p. 54-60.

the soul does not live in God. On a yet higher level of love it can be said that the soul that has attained God no longer lives either in itself nor in God; it no longer loves itself in itself nor in God; it loves God in itself. Finally, when God, the life and the source of all life, gives Himself to the soul and to living creatures, He does not live in the creatures but in Himself. While His being is supremely One, yet according to our way of understanding, the being of God in Himself is more perfect than that which He has in His creatures. Similarly, the soul that reaches the ultimate love no longer lives in itself nor does it live in God, nor does God live in it. That is because it does not love itself in itself nor in God; it does not love God in itself; it loves God alone—not God in the soul, but God in God. God is loved not for the sake of self, but only for His own sake, in the utter perfection of His being. The soul does not live in itself nor does it live in God, nor does God live in it: God alone lives in God. The soul loves neither itself in itself nor itself in God, nor even God in itself, but loves only God in God. This is the perfection of love: *solo Dio in Dio*.[5]

To understand better this absolutely pure love of God alone for God alone, we can eliminate all other objects of love. The human soul can love things inferior to itself and outside itself: wealth,

---

[5] *Schema, ibid.* p. 20; "Argumentation" III, p. 61-66.

pleasure, honors; it can love beings inferior to itself but united to it: the flesh and material life; it can also love what is equal to itself: its own self (loved for self or in God) and its neighbor's soul; it can love, finally, a being above itself: God in self or God in God. Only at this point does love become pure and perfect.

It is inevitable that such a chart of the degrees of love should be somewhat arid. To animate it, we find all the resources of a rich mystical vocabulary. An ineffable state can be described only by a series of vague but suggestive and evocative images or abstract ideas. The soul must penetrate into God, sink into the depths of God, be transformed in God, become submerged in Him.[6] This transformation is wrought by a blazing fire of charity in a furnace of love where the soul is cast to become utterly absorbed, consumed, and liquefied.[7] In the midst of these flames of love, the soul loses sight of its own self, dies to all self-love, becomes only pure love of God alone for God alone.[8] In this indescribable betrothal, God gives Himself by love and the soul consents to receive this divine communication. Just as two become one flesh by a physical marriage, so the soul becomes one with God by spiritual marriage. No longer are there two spirits, two beings who love, but, as it is written, "he who

---

[6] *ibid.* p. 51.   [7] *ibid.* p. 54, 59, etc.

[8] *ibid.* p. 64, 65, etc.

adheres to God is one spirit with God." Nothing is left but the life of God in God. The soul transformed in God no longer knows anything but God, no longer loves anything but God, no longer is anything but God.[9]

The soul that loves God in God is like an eye staring at the sun. It cannot see itself reflected. On the contrary, the more it looks and concentrates, the less it sees itself and the less is it capable of seeing itself. So the soul burning in the fire of God in God has no concern for itself. Its whole love is concentrated on God alone. No physical transformation can represent this fusion of the soul in God. Unlike what occurs when a substance burns and melts or when a drop of liquid falls into the ocean, this absorption of the soul in God does not cause the soul to lose its being in God. Indeed it acquires in Him a more perfect being. God's power and goodness can receive and assimilate without destroying even the smallest fragments of being.[10]

Divine love is a flame preserving even what it consumes: hence it is boundless. The more a soul is absorbed and transformed by love, the more completely it loses itself to acquire a more perfect self in divine love. As St. Bernard said, the limit of our love for God should be to love Him without limit.[11]

---

[9] *ibid.* p. 61-62.
[10] *Ragionamento IV*, p. 104-106.
[11] *ibid.* p. 109.

Although some persons may find this style too poetic or speculative, yet the underlying theology of love in all these pages is wonderfully practical. The touchstone of all true love is always detachment. No state or act of contemplation can be so sublime as to dispense with renouncement. To love God alone in God means to cling to nothing other than God Himself, to seek only God's glory. "How many there are who believe they are spiritual and wish to enjoy physical and spiritual rest in God— but not for the love of God, only through self-love. They prefer their false consolation to acts of obedience and fraternal charity. They are repelled by whatever deprives them of the rest they imagine they find in God but which they really seek in their own selves. Their whole concern is to find peace, not, it is true, in things inferior to themselves nor in themselves, but in God. Yet that peace is sought for self, not for God's glory.[12] On the contrary, souls that have attained perfect love no longer desire for themselves either virtue, or sensible devotion, or tears, or spiritual consolation or ecstasies or prophecies. If they receive such gifts they value them lightly; if they are without them they do not seek them, for it suffices to love God alone in Himself.[13]

"There are spiritual men who are considered saints and who rejoice in the progress of their Order or their monastery, but who in dealing with their

---

[12] *ibid.* p. 91.   [13] *ibid.* p. 97, 107.

neighbors are not exactly displeased by the neighbors' progress—for that would be sinful—but they are less pleased by it than by what concerns them personally. If they examine their attitude they will realize that they desire their own progress or that of their monastery more than they desire God's glory: they do not love God in Himself.

"The soul which rejoices in God and God alone is willing to be without any consolation. If its love of God could increase on condition that it be cut off from all sensible devotion, spiritual tranquillity, or joy—even on condition that it be deprived of all hope of such gifts in this life or the next—it would gladly agree to such conditions. It loves God no less when feeling no consolation or sensible devotion. The love of God remains the same whether or not He grants such gifts.[14] Could we even suppose a possibility of adding to God's glory by losing Him, rather then lessening His glory by possessing Him, then the soul consumed with love would prefer its own damnation for the sake of even the slightest increase of divine glory.[15]

To describe pure and perfect love Giustiniani does not flinch from such expressions, exaggerated though they may seem. He was sufficiently aware of the illusions of false mysticism to realize the danger of such notions: indeed he himself condemned the temptation of those who might wish to

---

[14] *ibid*. p. 110-111.   [15] *ibid*. p. 113.

be damned for the sake of God's love. But when he strove to show the demands of love he did not fear to permit such a comparison, as a mere hypothesis. Moreover, at the end of his "Argumentations," on the love of God for God's sake, he submitted his whole teaching "to the judgment, the dogmas, and sentiments of the Roman Catholic Church"—a gesture not without merit in Renaissance times.[16]

Rather than defend his orthodoxy, which is unquestionable, we prefer to recall that he himself was aware of the limitations of his language. He spoke mainly as a way of whetting his own desire for what he could not express. "Lord, I know that what I have tried to say, what You have enabled me to see and feel to some degree, is truly ineffable, unfathomable. . . . But grant, Lord, that what I cannot understand intellectually nor express in writing, I may taste and enjoy by experience. . . . Grant that I may be united to You in a way that the mind cannot grasp nor the pen express, that I may be so totally absorbed in You that I may love You and rejoice in You. I do not ask that your joy may enter my being, but rather that I, like the faithful servant, may enter into that joy, that I may wholly lose myself, be annihilated to myself and taste your love in a manner beyond all telling of understanding.[17]

---

[16] *ibid.* p. 116.
[17] *ibid.* p. 52-53.

XVI.

THE GIFT OF SELF

"There are two commandments of love, not just one. It is true that we must love God, but the Lord has also said that 'thou shalt love thy neighbor as thyself.' Therefore, he who loves only God in God seems to lack the fullness of true charity, since he concentrates all his love on God alone without directing any love on himself or on his neighbor. But the Apostle John has said that there is no love of God without love of neighbor. "If a man boasts of loving God, while he hates his own brother, he is a liar. He has seen his brother and has no love for him, what love can he have for the God he has never seen?[1] To develop a love directed toward God alone without any reference to oneself or one's

---

[1] I John 4:20.

neighbor: is not this the contradiction of all true charity?"[2]

A whole "argumentation" formulates the answer to this question. The solution of the problem is vigorously expressed at the very beginning in an invocation to Eternal Wisdom. "O God, who in one selfsame act love Yourself and Yourself alone while at the same time in Yourself as the adequate object of Your love, You likewise love all creatures, grant that I may understand and express how it is that souls that concentrate their entire love on You, at the same time love both themselves and their neighbors more than if they were dividing their love amongst You, themselves, and their neighbors. Show me how it is that when human souls are on fire with Your love, the less they heed self and neighbor, the greater becomes their love for self and neighbor. In this respect we may even say, paradoxically, that the less they love self and neighbor, the more they love them. Grant that I may understand and teach that if we seek to love self and neighbor, we must not deflect any part of our love from You, but rather we should desire to love only You. Souls will love self and neighbor perfectly only when they so strive to love You alone that they reserve no thought or love for self or neighbor, forgetting them as utterly as if they did not exist, giving them neither thought nor love.[3]

---

[2] "Argumentation" V, p. 117.   [3] *ibid.* p. 117-118.

Since God is supreme Wisdom, Goodness, Omnipotence, the best way to care for self and neighbor is to cast oneself and one's neighbor wholly into Him, to entrust them confidently to God, and then to think of Him alone, to love Him alone. Thus we may love self and neighbor more truly and more effectively than if we loved God less because some of our love was diverted to self and neighbor.[4]

However, the general principles of this answer require further explanation. Two comparisons help to elucidate it: the first concerns God's very being, the second, His love. While it is true that God's love is not different from His being, yet we may be permitted to distinguish between them for the purposes of explanation. If, therefore, we speak of God's essential being, we can say that God, by one and the same being, is in Himself and in creatures, the latter receiving a finite participation in His infinite being. But God is one being only: the being that He possesses in Himself is not distinct from the being that renders Him present to all creatures.[5] If it were possible for God to will to give up part of His being in order that by this part removed from Himself, He might be in His creatures, then He would not exist perfectly either in Himself or in

---

[4] *ibid.* p. 120.

[5] *ibid.* p. 122. This definition, while differing from those we are accustomed to find in classical theology, is by no means invalid, as Dom Stolz has observed. *Prefazione*, p. 17.

creatures. He is in creatures only by reason of being perfectly in Himself as the source of all being. Therefore He is in creatures only because He is perfectly in Himself. In like manner, the soul united to God by love, loving only God in God, not directing any love to creatures, is more truly and completely in God through love. Because it is wholly in God, it is by God's infinite being, in all God's creatures that are worthy of love. It is, indeed, more truly in them than if it willed to be less in God in order to belong more to His creatures.[6]

Let us now consider God's love and its object. God loves Himself, only Himself, Himself absolutely alone, as the only adequate object of His love. At the same time, in Himself He loves all creatures with perfect love. So too, souls that love God and God alone as the adequate and principal object of love, by that same love also love themselves, their neighbors, and all lovable creatures. They love creatures, not in themselves but in God. There is but one love in God by which He loves Himself and creatures. Were there two loves in Him, He would love neither Himself nor creatures perfectly. He can love only His own being and this love extends to all beings with which He shares His being. Similarly, in order that souls may love God, themselves, and their neighbors as perfectly as their limited capacity allows, they do not require two

---

[6] *ibid.* p. 122.

kinds of love. If their love were divided in two, it would be less perfect: whatever was directed to one object would be removed from the other. Their only love should be God in Himself. Love will then extend to all that God loves. This love of God alone not only permits the possibility of loving creatures but also determines how much creatures should be loved. The rule is to love creatures insofar as they are lovable in God. If we love God alone, we shall love creatures neither more nor less than God loves them and wants us to love them.[7]

This abstract explanation leads to practical conclusions. Since the act of love directed to God alone for His own sake is likewise bestowed on all lovable creatures, it follows that we must prove this love by interior and external acts of charity. Such love, that is based upon the love of God for His own sake, is sure of reaching others for God's sake, not for their own sakes. It will effectively help others to turn to God. The giving of ourselves to God in our neighbor will take on many different forms: rejoicing on the conversion of sinners, cooperating with penitents in their repentance by prayer and mortification, desiring that sinners be pardoned, suffering for the sins of others, praying and weeping for evildoers, offering to all men an example of the love of God, relieving the material needs of all whom we can reach, using every effort and desire and re-

[7] *ibid.* p. 123-125.

source towards finding others to supply such needs when we cannot do so ourselves.[8]

The result of the loving gift of self to all that God loves is the union of all creatures with God. The soul that loves God in Himself shares in the love by which God brings all creatures to union in love, while He at the same time respects their diversity. Here again a mystery is clarified by a comparison. One soul gives life to a whole living creature, conferring life on all its members by one vivifying power, yet informing each member differently, respecting, sustaining, and animating all the different functions. So also those who love God for Himself alone extend that love to all creatures loved by God, but bestow it on each creature according to its individual capacity, serving each of them by whatever deeds of charity each requires to foster union with God.[9]

The perfect model of this universal love is Christ who gave His life for the good and for the bad, for His disciples and for His persecutors, for His friends and for His enemies. Even those who were putting Him to death He saw in God and loved with the love that God had for them: their evil act did not change the fact they were creatures of God and shared His being and His love.[10]

The degree of love that God reserves for each of

---

[8] *ibid.* p. 129-130.   [9] *ibid.* p. 132-134.
[10] *ibid.* p. 140-141.

His creatures is known only to Himself. Christ knew it by divine insight, but men cannot penetrate the mystery. They have only to go to God directly; then, if they love God, they will love all that God loves and in the same way that God loves. So it is with the blessed inhabitants of heaven, the angels and the men who love God alone and for His sake already know in Him the degrees of love due to His creatures. When we ask in the Lord's Prayer that God's will be done on earth as it is in heaven, we express the desire to love God in Himself and all creatures in Him, loving as do the Blessed in heaven.

The love of God is a mystery which man cannot perfectly explain or understand. But sometimes men can experience it. When they burst into song in the joy that overwhelms their whole being. Blessed Giustiniani has left us a sonnet composed as a thanksgiving in the midst of such an experience. Annihilated and oblivious to himself, but at the same time united to the Lord, he sings of the thrilling joy that springs from his life with God.

"It is not surprising that my heart finds deep content and that my face shines bright with joy, for many times I sense and hear and greet the loved one who removes all pain.

"The Lord whose love I never wish to leave calls me and brings me to His very Self. His joy so thrills in every vein that even the memory of my own self fades.

"When my heart welcomes the Almighty and

dear guest, I cannot hide His visit as I wish. The glory of His presence shines even on my face.

This mighty Lord has not the habit of arriving in disguise to woo a lovely slave like me. How chaste our love is! How beautiful and full of joy!"[11]

---

[11] F II:115ᵇ.

Epilogue

XVII.

THE CROSS OF CHRIST
AND MARTYRDOM

Throughout his life Blessed Giustiniani longed for martyrdom. Often he pondered on whether he might journey to distant lands where he could bear witness to Christ among the infidels. He wished to bear testimony by silent preaching and by the example of an existence wholly consecrated to God.[1] When he understood that his vocation was the hermit life, he continued to view it as a "clear and eloquent testimony for Christ." "The more a man is honored in the world, the greater is the glory he renders God when his conversion leads him to the life of solitude, and the stronger is his testimony for Christ.[2] It pleased Giustiniani to read and to

---

[1] Cf. *Un humaniste ermite, op. cit.* p. 107, 112-113.
[2] Q I:211.

quote the texts where tradition referred to the martyrdom of those who adopted monastic life;[3] he liked the liturgical hymns that extol the martyrdom of confessors who, even without dying, endured voluntarily their slow mortification.[4] "In the time of the primitive Church, in the days of the tyrants, martyrs by their death confessed that Jesus Christ was the Son of God and that the Christian religion was the only path of salvation. Similarly in our day, in the midst of the tyranny of vices, amid crowds of men great or simple whose faith is vanishing, a Christian who could live in comfort but who, nevertheless, renounces the world, not from motives of weakness or discouragement—such a Christian truly testifies, by a voluntary martyrdom, that Jesus Christ is the true God, that our faith is right and true, that sinners cannot be saved unless they repent."[5] Eremitical life, more than any other, is a martyrdom because it implies more perfect forgetfulness of self: *sibi soli et Deo vacare*. But is there not a contradiction between this emphasis on oneself in God's presence and the desire to die to self in order to live for God and to love Him alone? *Solo Dio in Dio*. The contradiction is only on the surface, for to live *by* oneself does not mean *for* oneself. The soul lost in God receives from Him,

---

[3] F II:102ᵛ; Q IV:492.

[4] Q IV:492; *cf.* F I:100; Q IV:257; F I:155, etc.

[5] F I:54.

not from itself, all that gives it life: "*in seipsa, non tamen de seipsa, sed de eo qui est verum gaudium, vera quies, vera consolatio, Jesus dulcissimus.*"[6]

Jesus gives to the soul His peace and His suffering, or rather, His peace *in* His suffering. One of Giustiniani's last writings is an ardent proclamation of that true peace.[7] "Nothing can separate me from the charity of God in Jesus Christ. Will You deprive me, Lord, of the sweet delight I feel in loving You so much? I do not think so, for it is Your will that I should so love You. You may perhaps test me in order to know—or rather, to enable me to know —if I love You truly. So be it! Lord, test and try my heart; see if it contains any love but Yours, if it loves You otherwise than in and for You alone. Lord, destroy me and then restore me; lead me to hell and lead me back again; make me poor or rich, just as You please; humiliate me and then exalt me; kill me and then resurrect me; strike me and then cure me; should You make me die a thousand times a day, my love would be no less for You alone and in You alone. If You withdraw from me, leaving me like a barren, thirsty land; stripped of all sensible and present devotion or compunction or spiritual

---

[6] Q II:14.

[7] This has become the "Argumentation" VI in the *Secretum meum mihi.* p. 149-163. Only the outline was written for the seventh "Argumentation" which was to follow, p. 23.

consolation; deprived of all these delights that You
so graciously offer to my soul; despoiled of all the
adornments of the spiritual life, poor, naked,
wretched, abandoned—I shall still love You in the
same way and I shall know that You permit all that
for the sake of my own progress. What could You
possibly do, Lord—permit me to speak so boldly—
what could You possibly do to induce me to cease
loving You? Give me peace interior and exterior:
I shall love you. Give me war and battling, whether
interior or exterior: I shall still love you. Give me
consolation, interior or exterior: I shall love You.
Give me tribulations, aridity, anxiety: I think I
shall still love You. . . . Cast me into the flames of
purgatory and I shall love You, for they shall not
consume me, but will give strength and comfort
since they will lead me to You, my only love. . . .
Provided that I love You alone and not myself,
Lord, my treasure and my only love, I care not
what else may happen to me. Grant only that I may
do Your will and that Your good pleasure may be
totally fulfilled in me, on me, by me."

The soul thus at peace with God is at the same
time necessarily at peace with self and with all creatures. Where love is, there is peace. As a shadow
follows an object, so peace accompanies love—that
love directed, as we have seen, to all that God loves.
"The soul recollected in God is as imperturbable
as God. It is always peaceful. Men of the world love

things that change: therefore they well know that their peace lacks stability. But a soul in love with God cannot lose its peace, even in the midst of tribulation. In fact, true and perfect peace demands frequent facing of adversity, until the soul becomes so accustomed to it that trouble makes almost no impression. It finally finds suffering a source of joy. The soul consents to forego the Lord's visits, uttering neither complaint nor protest, realizing that the lack of sensible consolation is helpful to spiritual progress and necessary to salvation. Overwhelmed by trouble, it seeks refuge in none but God. Then only does it possess the peace of Christ, that peace that the Lord said He would give and leave to His followers. Christ called it *His* peace for every kind of peace is not His: the world's peace cannot be His peace.

Where is Christ's peace found? Only in His Cross, accepted voluntarily and joyfully. Our cross is the selfsame as Christ's: a cross formed by suffering from above, suffering from below, suffering from the right side and suffering from the left side. The suffering from above is our impression of being forsaken by God; from below, the attacks of the devil; from the right, the disdain of the angels and good men; from the left, persecution by evil men. That is the shape of the cross of our suffering. The soul enamored of God in this life not only does not spurn the cross, but goes to meet it, glad to carry it in peace and joy. Many men who think they have heavenly peace really rest in themselves or in the world. They lack true peace, which can never be found apart from the freely accepted and dearly cherished cross of Christ. He who seeks peace elsewhere deceives himself.

"Peace lies in desiring and accepting with joy all suffering, even if it be spiritual, in being unconcerned about temporal affairs. Eternal joys should be the object of all our desires, the target of our ardent hope. Peace does not mean a life of pleasure and consolation here below. We should be all the more pleased if our brief life brings greater suffering to make us more like Christ, more intimate sharers of His pain. For a servant of Christ no other peace can be called "peace."

"Happy the soul which attains that peace which never, never comes except by loving only God, and only for His own sake! O all lovable Lord Jesus, I beg You to give me peace and let it be ever peace with You. If I have that, then I surely shall have likewise, as far as possible, "peace with all men," as the Apostle says. If I am at peace with You, Lord, I can truly say with the Prophet: 'I was at peace with those who hated peace.' The soul that truly rest in the love of God alone, possesses a peace which nothing in the world can spoil. Neither attacks of sinners or insults of demons can in the least disturb that peace, for true love of God for God builds up a rampart that no force can shatter. The peace of Christ is a rock and an impregnable fortress. I may be attacked from every side but if I take refuge in Christ, I know that I cannot fall: I hope in God and therefore I shall be saved."[8]

---

[8] *Ibid.* p. 149-163, *passim*; *cf.* Ps. 26:3.

Appendix I
THE SOURCES

The doctrine of Blessed Paul Giustiniani is original in more than one respect. He was the first since the time of Peter Damian, at least in the Benedictine tradition, to assemble the elements of a coherent and complete account of eremitical life, expressed in a notably personal style. But little of his work is wholly new. He had no need to discover everything by himself, for the spirituality of monks and hermits had already been fully treated before his time. His strength derives from his enormous documentation in the best sources of general culture and Christian tradition.

References to the authors that he uses can be found in the *Index of Names Quoted*, p. 177-182 or the volume entitled *Un humaniste ermite, le bienheureux Paul Giustiniani* (Rome, 1951). This book will be referred to, in the rest of this Appendix, by the abbreviation *HE*.

Giustiniani knew the ancient Greek philosophers. He often mentioned Aristotle, but seemed particularly familiar with Plato (whose *Timaeus* he liked to quote) and Plotinus. His favorite Latin authors were Seneca and, more particularly, Cicero whose *Questiones tusculanes* played a role in his conversion.

The most important source of his religious though is undoubtedly Holy Scripture which he studied in the Greek text and in the Vulgate. He did not fail to consult also with those who knew Hebrew (*cf.* above, chapters 4-9.)

He was well read in the Greek Fathers, particularly Origen, St. Basil, St. Gregory Nazianzen, St. Gregory of Nyssea (*cf.* above Parts II and III and HE *passim*). In the Index of manuscripts at Urbino at the end of the fifteenth century (ms. *Urbin. lat. 1761, f.19*) there is a note regarding ms. n. 110: "*est penes fratrem paulum iustinianum uenetum.*[1] *Restituit.*" That manuscript, now *Urbin. lat. 46*, consists mainly of writings by St. Basil and St. Athanasius. (*Cf.* C. Stornajolo, *Codices Urbinates latini*, I, Rome, 1902, p. 51-54.) It is known that Giustiniani was acquainted with the Duchess Gonzaga of Urbino (*cf.* HE, p. 179, 192).

The Latin Fathers that Giustiniani quotes most

---

[1] The reading here is *uenetum* not *ueronensem*, the version of C. Stornajolo, *Codices Urbinates graeci*, Rome, 1895, p. lxxvii.

readily are St. Augustine (whose biblical commentaries he particularly admires), St. Jerome (whose Epistles he often read), St. Gregory the Great, St. Leo, and the Venerable Bede.

He absorbed the *Lives of the Desert Fathers.* Though he did not give the book his total approval in every detail (*cf.* HE, pp. 58-59), yet he considered it as one of the essential books for all hermits. When he noted what every hermit should keep in his cell, he gave this list of indispensable books. "a Bible, the life of the Desert Fathers, a Rule of St. Benedict, a Psalter." (FA 118ᵛ.)

He studied Cassian very thoroughly, reserving judgment on some theological points, (*cf.* HE, p. 172) but often relying on him with regard to the requirements of monastic and eremitical life.

He studied the Rule of St. Benedict, seeking the help of whatever commentaries were available (*cf.* HE, p. 63, p. 117).

He studied the Camaldolese sources. His desire for martyrdom was doubtless derived from the biographers of St. Romuald and Companions. He composed a whole volume of extracts from St. Peter Damian (Q V bis; *cf.* HE, p. 116). In drawing up his *Regula uitae eremiticae*, he was directly inspired by the *Constitutions of Blessed Rudolph.*

In the whole monastic tradition of the Middle Ages, the author with the strongest influence on Giustiniani is certainly St. Bernard. Several times Giustiniani told of the joy and profit he found in that saint (*cf*. HE, p. 177). He often quotes Bernard, directly or indirectly. Many of his fundamental ideas on the love of God, sometimes the wording of them, are inspired by St. Bernard, particularly the phrase above loving God without limit and the notion of loving God "in Himself and for Himself" (*cf*. *Breuis commentatio in Cantica ex uerbis s. Bernardi*, P. L. 184, 429 D), and also the ideas about the life of God in the soul. (*Cf*. above, chap. 15. *cf*. St. Bernard: In Cant. 81, 1-4, P.L., 183, 1171-1173.) St. Bernard's *De diligendo Deo* furnished some of the principal ideas of Giustiniani in his *Cogitationes quotidianae de amore Dei* (*cf*. HE, p. 148). Blessed Paul also composed a parable in the style of St. Bernard's: *Rex omnium potentissimus* . . . (F VII, 92). He states that he wrote it after reading a series of parables, this being most probably the collection of St. Bernard's parables (P.L. 183, 757-772).

Giustiniani made notes on St. Albert the Great and he praised St. Thomas whose opinions he sometimes rejected but whom he often praised as a reliable master, far superior to the professors of what he calls "the new theology," that is, "abstract theology without contact with traditional sources, as taught in Paris in the fifteenth century. (See above, Chap. 4, Part II. *Cf*. HE, p. 33.)

Giustiniani knew the *Decreta* of Gratian as well as the *Decretales*. He quoted from these works.

More than once he expressed his admiration for Dante and Petrarch.

Finally, one of the spiritual trends very close to him was the Franciscan spirit. He had great devotion to St. Francis and felt deep emotion whenever he passed near Mount Alverna (*cf*. HE, p. 177, 179). The original Franciscan spirit harmonized with his own tendencies in two respects: the yearning for solitude, and the yearning for poverty. Naturally therefore, he gave his approval to the first Capuchins (*cf*. HE, p. 125). It has been written very truly: "For the Franciscans as for the Benedictines, the primary and essential purpose was to *be* rather than to *do*. In this respect, the Benedictines and the Franciscans differ from other Orders such as the Dominicans, which were founded primarily for the sake of an external apostolate. It is true that the Franciscan vocation implies activity for the benefit of neighbor, as this is included in the evangelical ideal of life to which they were bound to conform to. But its principal purpose was to revive in its members the perfection of Christian life as portrayed in the Gospels."[2] It is difficult to determine, from the manuscripts preserved for us, to what extent Blessed Giustiniani influenced the first Capuchins and was influenced by them.[3] In any

---

[2] P. Cuthbert, O.M. *I cappuccini, Un contributo alla storia della contra-riforma.* (Faenza, 1930, p. 12).

[3] On this subject we have the studies published by Fr. Edouard d'Alençon, O.M. Cap. in the *Annales Capuci-*

case, certain similarities of detail in their way of dress and religious practices manifest the same desire to contribute to the reform of the Church and of monastic life by a return to the spirit of poverty and solitude.

---

norum, vols. XXV-XXXV, *passim.* Also especially valuable is the contribution of Fr. Burchard De Wolffenschiessen, O. M. Cap. *De Influxu legislationis Camaldulensium in Ordinem Minorum Capucinorum,* in *Collectanea Franciscana Capucinorum,* I (1931) p. 59-78.

Appendix II
EREMITICAE VITAE
DESCRIPTIO

The ideal of life presented by Blessed Giustiniani is perfectly illustrated by a very beautiful painting of El Greco, now kept in the Instituto de Valencia de Don Juan in Madrid.[1]

On the right, St. Benedict in a black cowl holds a crozier and a book that probably represents his Rule. On the left St. Romuald in a white cowl and with a long beard hold in his left hand a short plain rod and in his right hand a miniature image of the hermitage at Camaldoli.[2] Above these two figures is shown a hermitage surrounded by a thick circle of

---

[1] On the history and the interpretation of the picture *cf.* F. J. Sanchez Canton: *Catálogo de las pinturas del Instituto de Valencia de Don Juan*, (Madrid, 1923, p. 177-179).

[2] These same details are found in the engraving of the frontispiece to the 1520 edition of Giustiniani's *Regula uitae eremiticae.*

trees and topped by high mountains. In the center is a domed chapel; on the left of the entrance gate, a big building intended for commun utilities; in the forest, with thick rows of trees between each, are twenty-four cells with their gardens in front. This picture of a Camaldolese hermitage corresponds exactly to the description given by Yepes in the *Cronica general de la Orden de San Benito*, V (1615) p. 301 ff.

In a frame placed between the two figures there is the following poem, entitled *Eremiticae uitae descriptio*:[3]

O nimus felix sacra solitudo,
Quis tuas laudes valeat referre,
Vita, dulcedo, requies, asylum,
    Semita portus.

Antra deserti coluere sancti,
Montibus syluisque Camaldulenses
Nunc Eremitae satagunt beatam
    Ducere vitam.

Singuli plane rigide seorsum,
In suis cellis bene separatis

---

[3] The phrases at the beginning of the first and second stanzas are taken from the liturgical hymns of the Feast of St. John the Baptist, as found in the monastic Breviary. The second last line recalls the motto that St. Gregory the Great applied to St. Benedict: *soli Deo placere desiderans* (Dial., II, 1).

Iugiter degunt, comedunt, et orant
    Crimina plangunt.

Septies templum repetunt silenter,
Rite devote celebrant synaxim,
Ac Deum laudant, pariter canentes,
    Nocte dieque.

Si diu solus cupit esse quisquam,
Et frui vita penitus remota,
Is domi clausus remanet quietus,
    Celica cernens.

Regulam servant pietate multa,
Quam tulit Divus Benedictus olim,
Postmodum sanctus quoque Romualdus
    Ordinis auctor.

Hic Ravenatum procerum propago
Tesqua, vel saltus coluit rigentes,
Gratia, signis meritisque clarus
    Regnat olympo.

Appetant omnes nemorum recessus,
Labilis temnant bona cuncta mundi,
Eligant soli Domino placere
    His in Eremis.